No Good Deed

A FRACTURED FAIRY TALE
BASED ON A TRUE STORY

ROAN ST. JOHN

© 2019 Roan St.John
ISBN: 978-1-79-404833-1

In fairy tales, the princesses kiss the frogs, and the frogs become princes. In real life, the princesses kiss princes, and the princes turn into frogs.
Paolo Coehlo

Dedicated to Princess Denise and all the others who thought they were kissing a prince and wound up with a frog!

THE FANTASY: A SOCIETAL LIE

What woman of a certain age didn't grow up fantasizing about the handsome prince who would sweep her off her feet and whisk her off to a magical land where they would live happily ever after in a beautiful castle? I admit it; I loved those fairy tales about Cinderella and Snow White. As a little girl, there just didn't seem to be any downside to such a scenario, but what the hell did I know at the age of five? Not much. Fast forward forty years, two failed marriages, and several long-term relationships that were great until they weren't, and by then I had pretty much given up on this crazy idea of meeting anyone who even remotely resembled that prince of my childhood fantasies. Then in 1990, it happened. Yes, a real-life prince who had grown up in a palace in a faraway land, who was handsome, funny, suave, debonair, cultured, and cosmopolitan waltzed into my life, swept me off my feet, and systematically lured me into his fantasy world. In other words, it was the stuff of a young girl's dreams! For a while.

The fractured fairy tale I am about to tell has been reconstructed from journal entries, scraps of paper with thoughts and observations, scribbled notes in the margins of books and the backs of photos, flashbacks, nightmares, emails to friends and confidants, Facebook messages, and what I can dredge up from memory. Oftentimes, the most revealing information came to me during sleep as my subconscious constantly processed the actions of a man who sought to destroy me for his own pleasure and greed. After you've been used by a narcissist, your self-doubt is replaced by anger. *You* know the truth. *You* see how you were used, groomed, and brainwashed. Angry doesn't begin to describe how you feel. You may even want to murder the person who did this to you. You want to contact everyone they ever knew and tell them what they did. You will probably write them a letter and tell them to burn in hell. In the initial stages after your epiphany or having gotten away from this person, you will probably obsessively talk about it with your friends and family, so strong is your need to be heard and get the story get out there. For years you had no voice and were minimized and devalued that once you get a voice, you can't stop. I decided to write a book. This is not just my story; it is the same story that so many people tell about their experience. There are legions of us with a similar tale. If you can take comfort in anything, it's that you are not alone.

When I first met the prince, the term narcissism (or its sister term narcissistic personality disorder) wasn't even in our lexicon, except as it related to the Greek myth. We generally thought of a narcissist as someone who was overly concerned with their physical appearance. We didn't know that this term would come to describe an entirely different set of behavioral patterns and attitudes. Then there was the term "sociopath" reserved for the likes of Ted Bundy or Charles Manson or any number of hardened criminals who engaged in a lifelong pattern of crime and deceitful behavior. Because there may be some overlapping symptoms with Narcissistic Personality Disorder and Sociopathy, they are now listed under the umbrella of Anti-Social Personality Disorders, but are often simply referred to as "narcopaths," especially by the people who have survived their reign of terror.

If you think this can't happen to you, think again. The frogs disguised as princes are out there and they are searching for *you*.

HOW AND WHY WE GOT ENSNARED

Narcissists and those with APD (anti-social personality disorders) flock to highly sensitive people like bees to pollen. They have an innate sense about those of us who are authentic, caring, intelligent, empathetic, and trusting. They choose their targets well. They especially like independent, successful, resourceful, gregarious, and well-liked individuals. All the positive aspects of your existence make you the perfect victim and before you know it, those positive traits will become a thing of the distant past. There are countless articles on the internet that explain in great detail how and why we are chosen. They are but a Google search away.

What exactly is a personality disordered person? Let's take a look at some definitions to help explain their characteristics:

The DSM-V describes Narcissistic Personality Disorder as having these essential features: impairments in personality (self and interpersonal) functioning and the presence of pathological personality traits. The following criteria must be met: A. Significant impairments in personality functioning manifest by:

Impairments in self functioning (a or b): a. Identity: Excessive reference to others for self-definition and self-esteem regulation; exaggerated self-appraisal may be inflated or deflated, or vacillate between extremes; emotional regulation mirrors fluctuations in self-esteem. b. Self-direction: Goal-setting is based on gaining approval from others; personal standards are unreasonably high in order to see oneself as exceptional, or too low based on a sense of entitlement; often unaware of own motivations. AND

Impairments in interpersonal functioning (a or b): a. Empathy: Impaired ability to recognize or identify with the feelings and needs of others; excessively attuned to reactions of others, but only if perceived as relevant to self; over- or underestimate of own effect on others. b. Intimacy: Relationships largely superficial and exist to serve self-esteem regulation; mutuality constrained by little genuine interest in others' experiences and predominance of a need for personal gain. Pathological personality traits in the following domain: Antagonism, characterized by grandiosity, feelings of entitlement, either overt or covert; self-centeredness; firmly holding to the belief that one is better than others; condescending toward others, attention seeking, excessive attempts to attract and be the focus of the attention of others and admiration seeking. The DSM-V defines anti-social personality as this:

Failure to obey laws and norms by engaging in behavior which results in criminal arrest, or would warrant criminal arrest;

Lying, deception, and manipulation, for profit tor self-amusement;

Impulsive behavior;

Irritability and aggression, manifested as frequently assaults others, or engages in fighting;

Blatant disregard for safety of self and others;
A pattern of irresponsibility; and
Lack of remorse for actions (American Psychiatric Association, 2013)

Please keep these criteria in mind as I take you on a long, sordid journey of what life is like when dealing with someone who is suffering from either one or perhaps both of these personality disorders. A distinction must be made between personality disorders and a mental illness: A mental illness can be ameliorated by therapy or medication. That is not the case with personality disorders. It is generally accepted that they cannot be treated, nor can they be cured. It is estimated that approximately three percent of the population may be afflicted with these personality traits.

If you are reading this, and you see some similarities in your relationship, it's quite possible that you have encountered a personality disordered person. After talking to hundreds of other victims, we were always amazed that there were so many similarities – it was as if we had all been involved with the same person to varying degrees. What follows is my Fractured Fairy Tale and the struggle for survival in the world of chaos created by a personality disordered individual.

ONCE UPON A TIME

August 1989 – diary entry

What a fabulous day. I am giddy with excitement because I just bought a house – well, a summer cabin really – in a rural mountain community in Colorado! My very own house, not one I would have to give up in another messy divorce should I ever be so stupid as to get married again. It's small and unpretentious, only about 800 square feet, but it's certainly big enough for me. It has one large bedroom and a smaller room I could use as an office, a nice tiled bath, an efficient kitchen with brand new appliances, and a hidden washer and dryer. It had been gutted and completely redone inside so even though it had been built in 1959, it seems brand new. The best part is the twenty-eight-foot deck that looks out over the property and through the trees I can see the pond and the huge meadow with a stream running through the middle of it. And it's *quiet*; a type of quiet that doesn't exist in a big city. Although I am worlds away from the fast-paced life I have led in New York, Los Angeles, London, and Paris, strangely, I feel at home here. Unfortunately, it's only temporary because I still have the video and record projects to finish up in LA, so the most I can hope for, at least for now, is to be here during the project's hiatus, basically one week every seven or eight weeks.

My neighbors seem pretty welcoming and when I expressed concern about leaving my cabin vacant for long periods of time, my neighbor Sandra suggested that I rent it to her parents who were retiring and building a home nearby and needed a small house to rent during the construction process. I met with her parents, who were truly lovely people. Len was retiring from a long career as a bank officer for Wells Fargo. They had been anxious about finding a place to rent for the short-term that was not too far from their construction site but still close to their daughter. They were so excited about renting my little house because it solved all their problems, and gave me some peace of mind as well. We agreed on a price and signed a simple rental agreement for one year. Everyone was happy. I could now go back to Los Angeles and my hectic production schedule and not worry about my new little idyllic retreat in the woods.

September 1990 – diary entry – one year later
My tenants moved out and now it's time to set up my little cabin. It's been a logistical undertaking with me being in Los Angeles and having to do everything over the phone. It's a good thing I'm a producer because it took a lot of coordination to get living room furniture, a bed, and a few odds and ends set up for delivery the day after I arrive. I would have to sleep on the floor the first night, but that would be okay. Like camping, but in my very own little cabin. Production on the music video I'm working on ends tomorrow night. That means the next day, Saturday, I can be in my car at 7 AM and on my way to Colorado It's a sixteen-hour drive but I plan to break it up into two segments of eight hours each. I drove it non-stop a year ago, but good grief, that stretch of highway through the Badlands where there is

not a structure, gas station, or any sign of life for the entire ninety miles is a bit daunting and stressful. Better to have a leisurely drive, enjoy the scenery, snack on all the delicious road food I'm going to snag from Mrs. Gooch's, pack my favorite cassettes, check into the motel in St. George, Utah, have dinner in the restaurant (which actually has pretty good food), then a nice hot bath, and get a good night's sleep for the last eight-hour haul the next day.

This video project I've been working on has garnered the attention of one of the local news stations in Denver. They seem to think I am quite the celebrity because I am producing and repackaging the hip musical variety show of the Sixties. Both the TV station and the local newspaper want to do interviews with me and have asked that I come to the station one day next week at my convenience. This can't be anything other than great news because it means that the press will help keep me employed! And secretly, I'm flattered and just a bit overwhelmed by it all. In all the years I have been in the music industry, I never thought it was a big deal to mingle with rock stars or other luminaries. They were just people I knew or worked with. I sometimes find it intimidating that other people are in such awe of this part of my job and my life. But hey, I'll gladly do the interviews because as they say, "there is no such thing as bad press!"

Sunday evening – diary entry - Arrived in Colorado

Everything went as planned. I finished editing the video at midnight Friday, was starving after such a long session, so I stopped at the local sushi restaurant in Studio City for a quick bite before going home, collapsing, and mentally preparing for a long drive the following day.

The drive was spectacular! The beginning of the fall season was evidenced by the changing leaves and the crisp, clear air with the biggest, fluffiest clouds I'd ever seen over the countryside of Utah. There wasn't any traffic to speak of and after spending the night in Utah, I rolled into my driveway around 5 PM, stiff from sitting in the car for nearly nine hours. Thankfully, I had enough food left in my little cooler to have a snack without having to go to town and find a place to eat. All I wanted to do was sit on my deck and stare out at the pond in the meadow across the road and give thanks to the universe (*and* my ex-husband) for providing this beautiful place for me. Yes, the house had been an impulse buy, but I knew if I didn't invest the proceeds of my divorce settlement, it would get frittered away, and the settlement wasn't nearly enough for me to buy anything even remotely livable in Los Angeles unless I wanted to live in a shack in East Los Angeles, and maybe not even then! This little cabin is Martha Stewart cute and located in an area that was a refuge for people from Denver trying to escape the brutal heat in the summer. The road to the cabin had sold me before I even saw the structure. From the little town and the lake, the road wound through a narrow canyon and opened into a wide valley, at the end of which was a 14,000-foot mountain. The creek flowed through the meadow and along the road. It was a beautiful setting and I think I'd have bought the house no matter what it looked like. The most magical part about it was being able to go out on the deck at night and see all the stars in the pitch-black sky, something that was nearly impossible in Los Angeles. Tomorrow – Monday – I will call the TV station and make arrangements for the interview. Need to find a good hairdresser in town to give me a trim and maybe some highlights. Meanwhile, it's time to make my bed on the floor with the sheets and bedding I brought in the car, and get a good night's sleep. The real bed and a futon that doubles as both a sofa and a bed will be delivered tomorrow morning, and then I can start setting up house. I feel so optimistic about this change, although most of my friends in California think I have lost my freakin' mind. I hope they're not right.

The following Wednesday – diary entry

The telephone interview with the music reviewer for the major newspaper went really well. The article will appear in Friday's weekend edition as the cover story for the entertainment section. They wanted a recent photograph and thankfully I had one that was taken by the famous rock photographer Eric Hillson. It's nice to have friends to do those things for you. The TV interview won't happen until next week, so I have some time to relax and get acquainted with my new surroundings. Who knows what the future will bring as far as work goes. I know there are a couple of really well-paying production gigs on the horizon and having this house in Colorado will be my sanctuary from the crazy life I live in the entertainment industry of Los Angeles. Getting all this press here can't do anything but help my career. And as much as I hate to admit it, it's a real ego boost.

The following Thursday – diary entry

The interview at the TV station was an amazing amount of fun! Everyone was so nice and they treated me like a celebrity, which I thought was kind of funny. A couple of the camera crew were particularly interested in my prior marriage to the son of a famous record mogul and asked dozens of questions about the rock stars I had met during that time. The make-up artist dusted my face with a light reflecting powder, touched up my lipstick, and added a bit of eyeliner and then it was lights, camera, action! I was in and out of there in less than two hours and winding my way through Denver and up I-70 to my little cabin in the woods. It was nearly 8 PM when I rolled into the town and the blinking neon sign from a local, rustic-looking bar perched on the side of the creek caught my attention. It looked like something out of a Western movie. A nightcap sounded like a good idea because I was still on an adrenaline rush and knew I wouldn't be able to sleep for hours. It wasn't a weekend, so I figured it would be a quiet place to unwind. When I pulled into the parking lot there were a lot of Harleys outside, but hey, this was the mountains of Colorado. At least it wasn't horses tied up to the hitching post! And yes, there really was a hitching post. I went inside and the place was packed – with women! At least I think they were women, and then I saw the poster on the wall. Turns out it was Biker Dyke Night! Holy shit, it was like walking into a female Hell's Angels' bar. Everyone was dressed in their leathers and milling around from table to table. I couldn't have felt more conspicuous or out of place wearing Tiffany jewelry, designer jeans, cashmere sweater, Calvin Klein high heels, and carrying a Vuitton handbag. I was dressed for dinner at Spago; for a grubby Western bar full of lesbians who looked like they could wrestle a gorilla, not so much. Basically, everyone ignored me, thank God, so I took a stool at the bar and pretended to be invisible. The place was loud, smoky, and crowded but I didn't really care; I needed something to get me down to *terra firma* from the interview. I ordered a cognac, and sat at the end of the bar by myself watching the other customers in the reflection of the mirror behind the bar.

By the time I had finished my first drink, two guys walked in and sat down on the bar stools next to me. I nodded my head ever so slightly in acknowledgment and went back to my own thoughts. Out of the corner of my eye, I saw the guy sitting next to me sizing me up. I could almost feel his stare boring into my skull. (I'll explain about that emblematic stare later.) I turned my head to check him out. He certainly didn't look like one of the locals; in fact, he looked almost as out of place as I did. The guy he was with was talking in a pronounced Eastern European accent so he certainly didn't fit in either. My curiosity was piqued. I said a quiet hello. He was definitely interesting looking in an exotic way. He had very defined features, a broad and high forehead, and piercing green eyes. What I really noticed were his hands –

very elegant – and he held his drink with one pinkie finger extended. This was not some cowpoke. He was still staring at me with this penetrating gaze, then said, "You must be new in town. I've never seen you before."

"That's because I live in Los Angeles."

"Are you here on vacation?" he probed.

"Sort of."

"Are you staying at the inn near the creek?"

"No, I purchased a house here about a year ago and my tenants recently moved out. I decided this could be my getaway when I had a break from my rigorous work schedule."

"What is it you are working on and how did you wind up coming in *here*? This isn't exactly a place for chicks from LA." He swiveled around on his bar stool and nodded to the leather clad gorilla wrestlers.

"I'm a video producer and I'm editing a musical television program that was aired in the sixties. I just came from an interview at Channel 7 and I was still flying from the excitement so I decided having a drink would calm me down." His gaze became even more intense. I could've sworn he licked his lips.

Cognac does bad things to me. It makes me very talkative and relaxed, so we chatted about all kinds of things – where we'd lived, what we'd done, who we knew, and what plans we had for the future. When he asked me where I saw myself in twenty-five years, I replied that my dream had always been to live in Mexico and have a small farm where I could grow some of my own food.

His face lit up like a klieg light. "I have a farm in Italy. We grow everything there. Grapes for wine. Lots of tomatoes for sauce. Even some chickens."

"That sounds idyllic," I told him, surprised that he would have a farm in a country he no longer lived. "Do you get to visit often?"

"As often as I can. Are you married?" he asked, glancing down at my left hand.

"No. Divorced, and recently ended a year-long relationship with a descendant of that famous French chef. About the only relationship I have time for now is my job. It's an exacting spouse!"

As if on cue, he removed his leather bomber jacket to reveal a chef's jacket. He said he was a chef at the local Italian eatery and that he and his sous chef, the guy with the Eastern European (Polish, actually) accent had just stopped in for a drink after cooking for 150 people.

"The problem is when you cook there's no time to eat and now we're famished. And a little drunk! Do you live near here? By any chance do you have anything you could feed two hungry guys? Doesn't have to be anything fancy."

I thought for a minute. "Actually, I do. I have some grilled salmon and baby field greens, so I could whip up a nice salad. But I have to warn you – I am basically camping out in my house so I only have the basics; I don't even have a table and chairs we could sit on."

"Doesn't matter," he said. "We'll just sit on the floor. You'd be doing a good deed to feed two hungry chefs!"

So off we went in tandem. The two of them in the sous chef's car and me in the lead. It took about fifteen minutes to drive the canyon road at night. In that part of the mountains anything could be in the road – deer, elk, a fox, skunks, rabbits – so driving slowly was the only way to get somewhere in one piece. During the drive to my house, I started wondering if this was such a good idea. I'm not usually in the habit of inviting men I don't know very well to my house, but there was something about him that was very intriguing, and I hate to admit it, pretty damn sexy. But then I have always been a sucker for European men!

I made a salad of field greens, thinly sliced fried potatoes, crumbled salmon, and a *citronette* dressing. He was impressed. We sat on the floor in front of the fireplace in which he had built a fire with whatever wood was stacked outside. The Polish dude had fallen asleep on the floor. I opened a bottle of wine and we laughed and talked about anything and everything, but he never took his eyes off me. When I asked about his background, he told me, shyly, that he came from an old European family, and held the title of prince. I chuckled to myself that here I was in some remote mountain town and what do I run into but an aristocrat who could cook. By eleven o'clock I feigned complete fatigue and said I needed to get to bed. What I really needed to do was call my best friend Anna in Los Angeles. With the time difference it was still early there. I shooed them out the door and ran to my bedroom and picked up the phone to give Anna all the details.

She just laughed and said, "Only *you* would wind up in bum-fuck Wyoming meeting a real-life prince."

"Colorado! Not Wyoming."

"Oh, same difference," she said dismissively, "we all know there is no real world outside of Los Angeles. They're both as far away as you can get from Hollywood! You know, Roan, we all snickered when you bought those Tony Lama cowboy boots and dared to wear them to Le Dôme with your pant legs tucked in. All you were missing was a goddamn Stetson!"

"I'll have you know those boots cost more than a pair of Guccis, and were a fashion statement!" I protested.

"Sure, they were, sweetie, if you were herding cows in South Dakota!"

"Colorado. I'm in Colorado, not Wyoming and certainly not South Dakota."

"Doesn't matter. Not a one of us has any clue about this little town you've been prattling about. But truth be told, we all actually thought you'd come back to Hollywood with a cowpoke in tow and bragging about rodeos and bull sperm.

Leave it to you to meet a prince. You certainly do live a fairy tale life, that's for sure."

"We'll see about *that*! I've had my share of Eurotrash boyfriends – the ones with impressive backgrounds and titles and not a dime to their name that wasn't doled out from some kind of trust. At least this guy has a job, that's more than I can say for the Frenchie who also had some silly title that you can't buy groceries with and was always waiting for *maman* to put money in his account from Paris!"

"You only just met him so you're on the learning curve. Just take it slow. I don't have to tell you that, but I'm doing it anyway in case you've forgotten."

"You know me too well, but truly, dearest friend, he's so intriguing. Speaks five languages, is funny, elegant, intelligent, well-traveled, well, all the things that lure me in."

"Are you smitten?"

"Bedazzled is more like it. It's just such a shock to meet someone like that here – of all places. He's good looking, moves like a gazelle, has an engaging smile, and beautiful green eyes. Oh, Lord, Anna, I wasn't looking for this at all."

"You've only just met him so don't hop in the kip too soon, and make sure you get to know him."

"Yes, mom. I will do that!"

Ten days later approximately – undated diary entry

Production on the next video was due to start in three days not the week hence that I had been told, which meant I had to pack it in, close up the house, and get back in my car for the long non-stop drive to Los Angeles. My plan was to leave my house at six and pull into my driveway in Beverly Hills sometime before 11 PM, allowing a quick stop for gas and maybe something to eat at one of those eat-till-you-explode trough buffets in Las Vegas!

I saw the prince two or three times in the last ten days. He invited me to the restaurant as his guest and asked me what I would like to eat.

"Hmmm," I pondered, "how about risotto with *porcini* mushrooms, but only if the mushrooms are *fresh*." I was half joking about the fresh *porcini* – after all, I wasn't in New York or Los Angeles where they were easily found.

When he served me the plate of creamy, fragrant rice with beautiful slices of mushrooms, he demurely said, "I had to hike two hours into the mountains to find them. I hope you enjoy it."

I admit it, telling me he had trudged into the wilderness to find those mushrooms impressed me; and the meal was exquisitely delicious. As I was shoveling the risotto into my mouth I had to remind myself that this was how the French guy ensnared me – by making his great grandfather's famous dessert called *Pêche Melbe*!

We had quick drinks on two occasions after that. Basically, he was busy with the restaurant and I was busy in pre-production and on the phone for five to six hours a day. I enjoy his company immensely. We have so many common interests, but I made it very clear once again that I was not looking for a relationship because I was married to my job and had no time to devote to anything else. He seemed to accept that, said he was impressed by what I was doing and certainly wouldn't want to interfere, so things stayed light and friendly. We agreed to stay in touch while I was in Los Angeles. Yes, he made my heart flutter.

At 10:45 PM, I pulled into the garage of my small apartment in Beverly Hills, dragged my Vuitton bag and the little cooler up the stairs, and set them down near the door before flopping on my bed to stretch my back and legs. That sixteen-hour drive had nearly done me in. Driving at night was never one of my favorite things and the four-hour drive from Las Vegas in the dark through the desolate desert gave me pause and made me ask just what the hell was I doing? Everyone cautioned me that I was taking unnecessary risks by doing that alone. But risks never stopped me from doing anything because I didn't seem to possess that natural fear instinct that most people have. When I rolled over on the bed I saw the blinking light on my answering machine. I had checked my messages from a pay phone when I stopped for gas in Vegas and there were no messages. Who could've called? Well, well, well. It was the prince. I had to replay the message several times to fully decipher what he was saying because obviously he'd been drinking and his words were clipped and a bit slurred. "The night is clear, the stars are bright, and I love you." Oh, for fuck sake! How did a few casual get-togethers morph into this? All I had the energy to do was strip off my clothes, crawl under the covers, and go to sleep. I'd have to call Anna in the morning.

"Well, of course he loves you, darling," she cooed into the phone, after I told her about the message. "He's love-bombing you!"

"What do you mean?"

"Lavishing you with love and attention. I heard the term on Dr. Laura. And why wouldn't he love you? You're a beautiful woman, smarter than most anybody, independent, sophisticated, with a high-flying career, a house in the mountains of Montana..."

"Colorado!"

"Oh yes, of course, Colorado...an apartment in Beverly Hills, a new car, and lots of rich and famous friends. Need I say more? What's not to love?"

"Yes, but," I whined, "I haven't even slept with him, and he's only ever given me just a quick peck on the cheek. I admit I'm fascinated and yes, a bit smitten, but you know how leery I am."

"Come on, Roan, he's a prince! Where are you going to meet someone like that in the fast lane of Hollywood? You don't even want to hear about my disastrous dating life, and besides, it's not like he proposed. Let's have sushi before you go back to the seventh level of production hell and you can give me all the details of this burgeoning romance."

"But what if he turns out to be the Prince of Darkness? What then? I'm not anxious to get into another relationship. The last two nearly did me in. I'm quite content being attached to my job. At least it won't break my heart!"

"Don't be so pessimistic; that's not like you. You're normally so upbeat and positive that it's sickening sometimes. You always expect the best outcome of everything. Just go with the flow and see what develops. You have to admit it's a great romantic story!"

"Sometimes I get a twang that something's not right about this. Am I just being paranoid and overly cautious?"

"Yes, I think you are. Your instincts are clouded because of past disasters. Don't let your fears get in the way of a beautiful romance." Then she laughed. (She wouldn't be laughing if she heard the whole story now!)

Note to self: Never ignore your first instinct just because it isn't what you want to believe.

Ten days later – notes scribbled on a piece of notebook paper

I swear, this project is going to kill me. My production partner is jealous of all the press I got in Denver and feels left out, the execs at the record company are making noise about how I am overpaid and they could get a guy to do my job for less money (now *that's* a twist!), and my secretary, Fran, who weighs 450 pounds *at least*, is calling the rock stars in our Rolodex trying to sweet-talk their secretaries into giving her free tickets and backstage passes to their concerts. Some days are too crazy to even write about.

Diary entry - undated

Every morning when I roll into the office with my raspberry tart or chocolate croissant and a cappuccino, Fran hands me a pink slip that says "the prince called." The message is decorated with little hearts and a crown over the word "prince." Cute. There is never a number to call him back so I just toss the slip in the bin.

Production on this latest video is a special brand of hell. Studio time gets booked then canceled. My editor shows up late because he has to first watch *The Simpsons*. On one occasion when he was more than two hours late, (surely *The Simpsons* was over by now!) I called his house wondering where the hell he was. He yelled into the phone, "Jesus, Roan, I'm watching the war on TV!"

"War? What war?"

"They're *bombing* Tel Aviv!" he wailed.

"Oh, for fuck sake, there's nothing you can do about *that* so can you please get your ass to the studio so all this time I booked isn't charged to the project?" Sometimes I felt like his minder, not his supervisor!

The execs at the record company are bitching endlessly about costs, even though I am under budget. And the prince just keeps calling. Sometimes my secretary puts the call through to the studio, but goddammit, we are paying $125 an hour for an edit suite. I don't have time to gab on the phone, and made that perfectly clear to him, even if I was a bit curt, which I regretted after I hung up. But he wasn't here dealing with studio techs high on cocaine and knocking back shots of tequila. All I keep thinking about is this segment ending in four weeks so I can go back to Colorado where it's calm and peaceful. And spend some time with my new love interest.

Undated diary entry

Thank God for my acupuncturist/herbalist. Twice weekly appointments have prevented me from committing an act of violence that would be a swift end to my glamorous life as I knew it. After being stuck like a pin cushion, I stopped for some take-out lunch at Mrs. Gooch's and as soon as I opened the door to the condo where our office was located, I heard Fran say cheerfully, "Oh, wait! She just walked in the door." Fran clamped her fat paw over the receiver, and with a sausage-sized finger pointed to it and whispered, "It's your prince!"

I dumped my lunch in the kitchen and picked up the phone. Without even saying hello, I blurted, "Listen, I don't have time to talk because I have a meeting in an hour and still have to eat lunch then get over to the studio."

He said in a very quiet voice, "I have something to ask you." (I would learn much later that his quiet voice was a prelude to something nefarious.)

"Go ahead," I sighed, and he proceeded to tell me that he had a favor he would like me to do and that was to sell a cabochon emerald ring he has.

"You're in Hollywood, with all the high rollers; you probably wouldn't have any trouble selling it. I'll let it go cheap because I need the money to pay child support."

"Look," I said, a little annoyed, "I work eighty hours a week. I get up, come to the office, put in a full day's production work, go to the studio and work until midnight or two in the morning, go home, pass out, and get up the next day to do it all again. I really don't have time to try and sell an expensive piece of jewelry. Why don't you sell it there?"

"Oh, it's not the right market here for that kind of thing. I'm going to mail it to you, to the address on your business card. If you can do something with it, that would be great. If not, bring it back on your next trip."

I hung up the phone and thought, "What the hell?" Four days later a FedEx package arrived at my office. Wrapped in a piece of leather was an exquisite two carat cabochon emerald ring, set in yellow gold. I love emeralds, so of course I tried it on, but it didn't fit, so I wrapped it back up and tossed it in my production bag and promptly forgot all about it.

Nine days later – diary entry

One more week to go and I am out of this nut bin and on my way to my mountain retreat. I'm exhausted. Don't know how much longer I can keep up this schedule. The prince called the other night while I was in the edit studio. He sounded down, so I spent a half-hour trying to cheer him up, give him some encouragement, and console him over his restaurant woes. I always try to be supportive when people are struggling. My job as a producer is taxing enough and now I find myself worrying about the prince and wishing there was something I could do to cheer him up. I was starting to feel totally put upon. I have twenty-five people I interface with on a daily basis on this project and being perky and uplifting is the only way I can function and manage so many different personalities. But now I am preoccupied with all his troubles, and he doesn't seem to understand what it is I do or how much stress I am under. I told Fran to not put any more calls through to the studio when I'm working unless it's one of the execs from the record company or my production partner. He would just have to chin up and carry on until I got back to the mountains.

Undated diary entry

What a relief to walk into my little cabin in the woods and find it all neat, tidy, and clean as a whistle, thanks to my neighbor who offered to clean it while I was gone. I pulled the bottle of Armagnac from my bag and poured myself a stiff drink then went outside to sit under the stars. That lasted about ten minutes because it gets damn cold at night in Colorado at 8000 ft. It was too late to light a fire so I flipped on the furnace to warm things up and ran a hot bath. After a half dozen trips here, it is starting to feel familiar and a bit like home, although I doubt that I will ever live here full time. This is just the place I escape to from my real life of craziness in the fast lane.

The following day the prince called and asked about the ring. "I have it," I told him. "I'll give it back to you the next time I see you." He went quiet. I heard him heave a deep sigh. I asked what was wrong. He said he really needed to sell it. I told him he could certainly do that after I returned it. Another awkward silence.

"Look, could you do it here? There's a nice jewelry store in the shopping center. Take it there. But don't tell them where you got it. Just say it was something you inherited from an uncle or your father and you want to sell it. Take whatever you can get for it. My ex is hounding me about child support."

This was getting complicated, and why I agreed to do this still remains a mystery. Maybe I just felt sorry for him. He had told me that his ex was a demanding bitch and was always hounding him for money. I assumed he was telling the truth. (And only after waking up in the middle of the night in a cold sweat six months after our divorce did this finally make sense.)

The next day I went to the jewelry store where coincidentally I had had my own emerald ring repaired on my previous trip, and spoke to the owner. I showed her the ring and told her that I had inherited from an uncle who had recently passed, and as much as I loved the stone, I really should just sell it and what did she think I could get for it. I wasn't comfortable telling that lie but she bought it and said she would need to send it to the local gemologist to get an appraisal and she'd get back to me. Two days later she called and said she could give me $800 in cash. I agreed, went there that afternoon, picked up the money, and dropped it off at the prince's restaurant. I was in a rush to get home to do a conference call so I didn't make chitchat, just gave him the cash in an envelope, and left. I had bigger things to worry about – namely, the next project, because the one I was working on was winding down and the only reason I was able to afford my lifestyle was that my salary was outstanding! Without that, I would have to think about renting out the house in Colorado. I wasn't sure I could find another gig in Los Angeles that paid me as well, and I certainly didn't think I could find something to do in my little mountain town. Let's face it, it wasn't LA and the jobs I was used to simply didn't exist there. I started to panic.

Meanwhile, the prince lost his job at the restaurant because the owners had sold it and one of the new owners hired another chef. This prompted the prince to look for other opportunities, and the one that seemed to make the most sense was starting his own restaurant, getting a couple of partners to finance it, and move on. It certainly seemed like a good idea; after all, he was a great chef and had quite a local following. There didn't seem to be any downside to this idea, other than taking in partners. Nonetheless, he persisted and teamed up with a couple of people who also liked the idea. It was a go! He was insanely busy and I rarely saw him, but we talked on the phone for hours, and as much as I tried not to, I was falling for him – hard. He always seemed to say the right things and he was so supportive when I bitched about my own work woes. But with our crazy schedules it didn't seem possible that this romance could flourish. And of course, I was always dashing back to Los Angeles on a moment's notice. I was usually in Colorado for ten days to two weeks and then four weeks in California before heading back to Colorado. The whole routine was exhausting.

Two months later

"It's a shame you haven't ever had time to see more of Colorado. It's really beautiful and the nature is outstanding. I have a friend in Aspen who invited me down next week. Would you like to go?" He was his most charming self and although it sounded like a good idea, I balked, saying I didn't have time. I had to be back in LA in about twelve days and all I really wanted to do was nothing. But he persisted, saying it was a beautiful, relaxing drive, plus we had a place to stay, and I could even have my own bedroom so I wouldn't think he had untoward intentions. I told him I'd think about it and let him know. When I found out the production schedule was pushed back for an additional five days because certain rock groups were hesitating about participating in the video series, I got so fed up with the whole scenario that I decided a change of scenery was just what I needed. Of course, we would take my car, which was only a year and a half old, (the car he drove could only be described as a beater reject!) and I offered to pack road food so we didn't have to stop on the way because something told me I'd be paying for that if we did. I bought all kinds of healthy food items for sandwiches and snacks, filled up the gas tank, checked the oil, and when he called later that day, we made arrangements for me to pick him up in the morning – not where he was actually living, but at the restaurant. That seemed strange to me, but he said that there were four or five rooms upstairs that were furnished as bedrooms and that he often spent the night there after the restaurant closed. The rest of the time he said he lived in a studio on the other side of town, which he confided reluctantly was actually part of his ex-wife's house.

So off to Aspen we went. I drove most of the way while he regaled me nonstop about his adventures in Italy, Pakistan, Afghanistan, India, Sardinia, France, England, New York, Los Angeles and all the fabulous restaurants he had opened all over the world, and how he was one of the best chefs to ever walk in a kitchen. It was a hard sell, that's for sure, and I was intrigued, but in the back of my mind was this question: "If you're so famous, why aren't you rich? And why don't you have your own place to live and drive a decent car?"

His friend was nice enough, and had a big apartment. The prince said he would sleep on the sofa and I could have the spare bedroom. We walked around town, ducked in and out of all the quaint shops, then went to the local market and picked up some things for dinner, which he paid for. He made a fabulous dinner and I was stuffed with some of the best food I had eaten outside of LA or New York. Afterwards, he said there was an historic bar in town that I *had* to see, so off we went for drinks. After three or four drinks each, he stroked my arm, leaned in (he was quite plastered by now), and said, "Can you pay for this? I left my wallet back at the apartment."

How we drove from the center of town to his friend's place is a mystery considering we were both drunk. We quietly went inside, sat on the sofa, and he turned on the TV. I was ready to go to bed being drunk as I was, but there on the screen was some torrid love scene, which he took as his cue to start kissing me. Okay, so one thing led to another and we wound up having sex on the living room floor. I had rug burns on my butt the next day so it must have been quite passionate, although I had no memory of it at all. I definitely felt that he had deliberately plied me with alcohol (which I paid for), to break down my defenses. I needed to talk to Anna. She'd get me straightened out. Two days later we were back in our town. I dropped him off at the restaurant and I went straight home and called my counsel.

"Okay, so you had sex on the floor. It was probably better than some of the places you've had sex, like the bathroom at The Peppermint Lounge or was it CBGBs, so don't make such a big deal out of it. You haven't had sex since you broke up with Frenchy so count your blessings. Was it at least fabulous?"

"Hell if I know. If the rug burns on my butt are any indication, then I would say yes, but we were both drunk and my memory is pretty dim!"

Over the next couple of months, the prince and I saw one another fairly regularly. Between his work schedule and mine, that boiled down to maybe twice a week. He often didn't spend the night but went home – wherever home was at the time. In between seeing him there were always long, long phone calls that went on for hours. We were definitely forming a strong bond, and he really was very sweet and concerned about my hectic work schedule, but sometimes after these long conversations, I was completely enervated, and would think to myself, "This is nothing but a big distraction." But the love bombing Anna told me about was still coming – how much we had in common, how he felt so comfortable with me, how he'd never felt like this before, how maybe we were true soul mates and were destined to be together. I'd never heard a pitch like that and I'd had two previous husbands and a fairly extensive list of lovers both long and short-term. Before long, I started to believe him, although it had never once occurred to me that there was such a thing as "soul mates."

Soul mates or not, he had annoying habits. Schedules meant nothing to him, nor did specific times that we had agreed upon. He pretty much came and went as he pleased, and at first, I was fine with that. Until it started to interfere with my life.

"This is not working out," I whined to Anna late one night. "I think I have to put an end to it once and for all."

"What's the problem?"

"He comes and goes as he pleases. Says he will call and doesn't. Says he is coming over after work but never shows up. The only way I can reach him is at the restaurant because he doesn't have his own phone at his ex-wife's house."

"Uh, sweetie, I hate to mention the elephant in the room, but why the hell is he still living with his ex-wife?"

"He says he lives in the studio, but I think it's really the garage. And sometimes he stays upstairs at the restaurant where there is no phone."

"*That* doesn't sound very stable or promising. Maybe you're right to think about ditching him. Or, maybe he should just move in with you. It could solve two problems – give him a place to live and give you some rent income while you figure out your next job situation. Plus, you'd be doing a good deed."

"Good deed? I'm not an aristocrat rescue mission. Besides, you know damn well what they say about 'good deeds'. Not only are they unappreciated, but you are often punished for doing them. The big problem is that I have fallen for him. I didn't think I would but putting all the negatives aside, he is really interesting, and smart, isn't overweight – you know how I feel about *that* – and he is quite amusing. On top of that, he can cook!"

"Well, Roan, eventually, you need to take a leap if you're ever going to find happiness in a relationship. He does sound like Prince Charming when you point out those things."

"I just hope he doesn't turn out to be the Big, Bad Wolf. And you're one to talk about taking a leap given that you are constantly extolling the virtues of single life. Besides, I *am* happy. And I want to stay that way."

"Suit yourself, sweetie. I'm just trying to give you some encouragement. I know you have this fear about getting hurt again, but that's just part of life. And who knows, maybe this *is* the stuff of fairy tales and you'll be living happily ever after."

Undated diary entry

For the last couple of weeks, I find myself thinking about him and wondering how it could be that I finally found someone who really shares my interests, political views, aspirations, dreams, and plans for the future. I admit I am totally enamored, thinking this is just too perfect and then wondering what I'm not seeing. I keep looking for clues that it's not real, but then I find myself hoping and praying that it is. I had not expected to meet someone so perfect at this stage in my life and had resigned myself to just being alone until I died. Maybe I have a chance at happiness with the prince. He certainly says everything a woman like me wants to hear so I kick myself back into reality when doubts start to creep into my thoughts. There is nothing that says I have to rush into this relationship and I have a firm footing financially now with owning my house, making a ton of money, investments, etc. I don't need a man to enhance my lifestyle; I need a man to share my life and dreams. I want a partnership where we are both working toward a common goal – and that is a well-ordered life, free of stress and financial liabilities. A relationship based on trust and mutual respect. It's too soon to tell how any of this will work out, but I am willing to give it a chance.

Over the last few weeks, he had been leaving a few things at my house – a tooth brush, a change of clothes, a few odds and ends. It seemed like the next step was for him to move in completely and share the expenses on my house, which would take a burden off of me until I lined up the next gig. I didn't come right out and ask him if he wanted to do that because I had decided to wait and see what happened in the coming weeks, and it didn't take long before things got dicey.

"A really old friend of mine is in town and I think you will enjoy meeting him. What if we came over around six o'clock and have some dinner and spend an enjoyable evening on my night off?"

"Sure! I'll make dinner. See you tomorrow!"

Six o'clock came and went as did seven and eight. By ten, I was pissed and disgusted. This was the last straw. I put the dinner I had made in the fridge and went to bed fuming. The next morning, I got up, grabbed a big trash bag, filled it with whatever he had left at my house, tied a knot in the sack, and put it outside on the deck. Still not a word from him. At three in the afternoon, he sauntered up the stairs with his friend in tow, laughing and speaking rapidly in Italian, and saw the bag. He called to me in a frantic voice and banged on the front door. I opened it and just stood there.

"Yes?" My arms were folded across my chest and I knew I had on my pissed off face.

"Wh-wh-what is *this*?" he stammered, pointing to the bag.

"Your stuff."

"But what does that mean?"

"It means that I am not running a fucking hotel where you can come and go as you please, whenever you want, saying you'll show up at a certain time – such as last night at six and it's now three in the afternoon the next day. I'm done. This is over. You need to take your stuff and leave."

Meanwhile his friend was standing there slack-jawed and wondering what the hell was going on. The prince pushed his way inside, took me by the hand, and led me to the little room that I had set up as an office. He put his arms around me and pulled me close.

"I am so sorry. Please forgive me. Robert and I started talking and drinking and the next thing I knew we were drunk and it was too late to call you, but I'm here now. Let's not fight. You are over-reacting and making a big deal out of nothing. I specifically said that I would *try* to come over around six. Obviously, you misunderstood me or simply took it all wrong. I never said I would be here for *sure*."

"I don't think I misunderstood anything! I told you I would make dinner and you said 'that would be great'. How was that not a definite plan?"

He just shrugged and gave me a blank expression that turned into this devious little smile. Then he kissed my neck and whispered in my ear.

"You know I care about you so much, and I promise I will never do that again." (Well, not until the next time anyway. And that was my introduction to gaslighting.)

I relented and thought maybe I *had* been unduly harsh and reactive, and maybe even misunderstood what he had said. Had he really said he *might* be over at six? He convinced me that it was silly to get so upset about something so minor. Even as he was soothing me, I was seething inside and feeling totally disrespected. I wanted to believe him; I wanted him to be sincere about being sorry I misunderstood him. But had I? I replayed the conversation over and over in my head as he held me tight against him and to be honest, I just wasn't sure anymore although it wasn't like me to misunderstand something like that. I'm generally very precise and careful about interpreting verbal cues, and despite any reservations I had, that didn't stop things from moving forward.

Within a couple of months, he was living full time in my house. We had agreed that he would pay half the mortgage, which at the time was relatively small and there was no place he could rent anywhere else for that amount of money. But he never seemed to have the money for the rent – or anything else. He was always hitting me up for five, ten, or twenty dollars with the promise that he would pay it back. Meanwhile, my video gig in Los Angeles had ended. I now had to scramble to figure out what I was going to do for income. I didn't have to scramble for long. Early the next morning I got a phone call from Aaron S., the computer mogul who had organized the largest concert since

Woodstock. It had been videotaped and he now wanted to turn it into a series much like the one I had just finished. He wanted me to come to Los Angeles for a meeting as soon as possible. Needless to say, I was thrilled. I made a plane reservation for four days hence, arranged for a rental car, and called my former secretary to see if I could stay in the guesthouse of the estate she lived on. She said okay, so I started packing for the five-day trip back to the concrete jungle. One of the things I needed to pack was a bit of pot to smoke when I got there. I had brought some very high-end marijuana with me on the last trip and since I rarely smoked anything at all, I expected to find a nearly full one-ounce bag in the drawer where I had stashed it. Imagine my surprise when I pulled out the baggie and it contained only dust. I scowled at the prince.

"Did you smoke *all* of this?"

He waved his aristocratic hand in the air to dismiss my question. "What's the big deal? It's only a bag of pot!"

"That cost $400 an ounce!" I groused.

"All you care about is money," he sneered under his breath. "When are you leaving? I'll get you some before you go. It won't be so exotic, but it will be just fine."

I had told him in the very beginning that I had seen my share of drugs when I lived in New York, and that I didn't want anything to do with either cocaine or heavy marijuana use. We see how much attention he paid to that!

The trip to Los Angeles was great; my meeting went swimmingly, and Aaron cut me a $5000 check to get started on the clearances, which pretty much entailed contacting every major musical group of the Eighties. I was on the phone from morning till night. It was exciting to be working on such an historic event. The problem was I'd be on the phone with some famous rock star's agent or lawyer negotiating terms and my call waiting function would beep.

I'd interrupt the call to see who's on the other line. It almost always was the prince's ex-wife demanding to talk to him. One day she called twenty times. I couldn't get any work done like that, so I finally just stopped answering call waiting. I informed the prince that this was not acceptable; that whatever his problems were with her, he needed to tell her to stop harassing me. He would mutter something in another language, storm out the door, and return many hours later, drunk as a skunk. This was not working for me. I told him that the situation could not continue; that my career was being railroaded by his messy divorce, and this was not what I had signed up for. He promised he would talk to her but he claimed she was just an unreasonable bitch and was never happy with anything, and that's why they'd split up. I told him it didn't matter to me what happened between them; I would not tolerate this kind of disruption in my working life and he had to straighten out their issues. Things did settle down after that, and by the third or fourth week of working fourteen to sixteen hours a day, I needed a break. He suggested we go to Ojo Caliente, a hot springs just outside Santa Fe. That sounded fabulous, so I got on the phone, made a reservation, packed some road food, and told Aaron I was going to be gone for three days. He agreed that I needed this retreat. The prince said he would spend the night at the restaurant rather than coming home because he had some last-minute ordering and prep to do at the restaurant if he was going to be gone three days. He said I should pick him up there early the next morning since it was on the way to the highway we were taking anyway.

I got to the restaurant at eight o'clock. He literally flew out the back door, opened the driver's door and demanded to drive my car, got in, and sped off. His face was pinched with anger.

"What the hell is the matter? You're acting very weird and look totally pissed off."

"That bitch ex-wife does nothing but demand money from me. I could've gone back to Italy and had a wonderful life but I stayed here for my daughter. I made all the sacrifices, but the bitch just won't let up! I need to calm down, and don't want to talk about it anymore. Just let me drive."

The tension in the car was palpable, so we drove in silence. Twenty minutes later we reached the main highway and he took off like a rocket.

"Hey, slow the fuck down," I yelled, but he waved his hand to dismiss my concern and continued driving at breakneck speed. I was gripping the door handle so tightly that my hand cramped. Wouldn't you know it, I saw a State Trooper behind us in the side mirror. "Pull over. The cops are behind us with flashing lights!"

He muttered a string of swear words and found a safe place to pull off the road. The cop was nice enough but it didn't stop him from issuing the prince a speeding ticket for doing 85 in a 50 mph zone. The remaining drive to Santa Fe was tense.

We got to Ojo Caliente hot springs and I checked us in. We went to our room, which was a bit rustic but then so was the whole resort. I was all eager to get in the hot pools, have a nice meal, maybe have sex, and enjoy the time away from the stress of pre-production. He only wanted to lie in bed, smoke pot, and watch CNN. I went to the hot tubs by myself. I came back a couple of hours later and he was in the same position. I suggested going to the restaurant to get dinner. He wasn't interested. I begged, saying, "Hey, this was your idea. Let's have some fun. Come on, I'll treat." (I had already treated by paying for the room.)

"You go. Bring back something."

"Oh, come on," I pleaded. "I went to the tubs by myself and let you sleep and chill out but now you're just ignoring me, as if I don't exist."

He turned to face me. "I'm sorry. The fight with my ex really upset me. I don't mean to take it out on you. But I have a headache from driving, so just let me lie here."

I was pissed. I went to the restaurant, ordered fresh trout for dinner, got the same dinner to go for him, and went back to the room. He was sleeping but woke up when I came into the room. "I brought you a trout dinner," and moved closer to hand it to him. He rolled over, away from me.

"I don't feel like eating. Just put it in the fridge. Maybe I'll eat it later."

I put the dinner in the little fridge and crawled in bed to watch some TV. He ignored me. The next day he was all apologetic, and a totally different person, upbeat, smiling, excited. "Let's go for a scenic drive around Santa Fe. It's a great little town. We can have lunch, do some shopping, what d'ya think?" I couldn't believe the change in his attitude and behavior. He was back to being wonderful and fun, and affectionate, too. I was so happy!

Since I'd paid $500 for this excursion, I figured I should at least see some of the surrounding area. It had been a long time since I was in New Mexico and I was eager to see some familiar sites. He finally mellowed out and we had a great time, but I couldn't help but notice that he was prone to wild mood swings with very little prompting. When I queried him about that, he blamed it on his ex, said he would try to not bring his troubles to our relationship. I said that was a good idea. But worse than all of that, I was feeling the beginning of a urinary tract infection. We had sex two days ago, and I was fine, but now I needed to find a big jug of cranberry juice.

Back in Colorado, I continued my pre-production work and he spent most of the days from early in the morning until late at night at the restaurant. He said they were preparing for the grand opening and that there were still lots of things to work out. He gave me the date of the opening and said it would be a gala affair. I was looking forward to it.

The opening night came and I got dressed up and went to the restaurant. I walked in to a packed house and found a seat on the sofas in the bar area. Much to my surprise, his ex was sitting on the sofa across from me. Instinctively, I said hello, put out my hand, and said, "It's a pleasure to meet you." She scowled, ignored me, got up, and stormed into the kitchen, and yelled at him. I waited for a lull in the tirade before I went through the swinging doors and asked if I could have the bottle of champagne I had given him earlier in the day to chill. He told me to get out of the kitchen and go sit down. He pointed to the reach-in where the champagne was so I grabbed it and went back to the bar area. I could sense that things were pretty tense, so I only stayed a little while and then went home, having no interest in witnessing this kind of chaos. I did notice that his ex seemed many years older than he was, and she didn't look happy, as if the scowl had been permanently etched on her face. If I had to describe how she looked it would be completely worn out. (I would become very familiar with that look!)

He didn't come back that night; I assumed he had stayed at the restaurant. He could've called; he knew how much I hated his disappearing acts. We agreed the next day that he should stay there until he sorted things out. It didn't take long – he came back to my house within three days with his tail between his legs apologizing profusely, and promising not to let his ex interfere in our lives.

Fast forward to the holidays.

It was almost Christmas, and we had been invited to a mutual friend's house at two o'clock for dinner. The prince told me he had to go to his ex's house in the morning for a family brunch and that he would be back by one at the latest. Nope! Two o'clock came and went. So did three, four, and five. At five-thirty he rolled in with no reasonable explanation and insisted he was ready to go to dinner.

"We're three and a half hours late," I pointed out.

"So? What's the big deal?" he protested. "Are you coming or not?"

I just stared at him, equivocating about what to do. After sitting around for more than three hours waiting for him to return, I was too agitated and stressed out to think straight. I instinctively blurted, "NO!" turned on my heels and walked into my bedroom and slammed the door. Seconds later, I heard his car pull out of the driveway. So there we were. Our first Christmas together, ruined. I was so upset that all I could do was lie in bed and cry. (It would be the first of many ruined Christmases, birthdays, Thanksgivings, Easters, Valentine's.)

Happy New Year – diary entry

A crushing disappointment came when Aaron called and said that the project was now on hold. The master tapes were in legal dispute and the only thing to be done at this point was to do nothing. So there I was without a high-paying gig. Thankfully, I still had some money saved. I decided not to fret. But I was not comfortable in that position so I started brainstorming about what I could do next that would keep me afloat.

Several weeks later, I got the bright idea that the country band a friend of mine started in Los Angeles might have some potential in Colorado. I contacted the former drummer of a famous rock band who just happened to live in the same town and who owned a recording studio. I told him what I had been doing. He was intrigued (and also between projects) and after many discussions and listening to tapes of the songs recorded in LA, we formed a partnership for the purpose of producing a record with the band. It all seemed to be working out.

My partner owned a high-end recording studio where we worked on the record. It was tedious and stressful getting musicians together, booking gigs for the band, laying down tracks, calling in favors from other famous musicians to play on the tracks so we could keep production costs down. During the day, I was doing the publicity and booking gigs for the band. At night I was in the recording studio. I was only home to sleep. The prince was working long hours as well, so we became like ships in the night. I would usually get home around eleven and he would roll in around midnight or one and crawl into bed, but he tossed and turned so badly that I rarely got any good sleep. He claimed it was just a stressful period right now; that normally he was a very peaceful sleeper. He assured me that he loved sleeping with me because he felt so close and happy. But for whatever reasons, we'd pretty much stopped having sex with any degree of frequency. It was down to once a week at the most and the blame was always laid on our busy schedules and the stress factor. Plus, there was always an adjustment period when two people begin living together, he claimed.

DISTRESS IN THE TOWER

Let's put it this way: Before there was Martha Stewart, there was my mother - a domestic goddess of the highest order. She taught me from the time I was five years old that a woman's house must be totally organized and neat at all times. Linen closets were for the proud display of carefully folded sheets, pillowcases, and towels. Everything must be lined up and stacked perfectly, even though nobody ever looked in anyone's linen closet, did they? The same applied to kitchen cupboards. Spices must be alphabetically arranged, dry goods must be organized and grouped together, jars of pasta, beans, rice, and other grains were to be in glass jars clearly labeled. Same went to the silverware drawer and the utensil drawer. There could be nothing out of place if you were to run a well-managed household. Having been totally brainwashed about these issues, I did in fact have a very organized and neat house. As obsessive as it sounds, there was something calming about knowing where everything was and everything having a place. But little by little these things came undone after the prince moved in. Things were stashed in the linen closet any which way. Sometimes I would open the door and the towels would tumble out. Food items were put in any cupboard where there was room. It didn't matter where anything went. The utensil drawer became the place where he deposited beer caps, rather than put them in the trash, which was not two feet away. Rather than complaining, I simply put everything back in order until it became too unmanageable. The first time I asked if he could please put things where they belonged, he completely ignored me and walked out of the room as I was talking. I assumed he got the message, but alas, several weeks went by and the problem persisted. I brought it up again and this time I was more assertive.

"I don't want to make a big deal out of this, but I am not comfortable with your undermining my organizational skills. I quite like having things neat and orderly because I simply do not have time to continually put things back where they should be. Could you *please* try a little harder? I would really appreciate it." The whole time I was talking to him, he averted his eyes and even turned his back on me. His response was to throw his coffee mug into the sink, mutter a string of expletives in Italian, storm out the door, returning eight to ten hours later, or sometimes not at all. This was starting to be our new normal. Each time he returned we acted as if nothing had happened. The previous weekend when he disappeared, I found myself getting in my car at ten-thirty at night and driving to town to check the local bars to see if he was there. Not only did I feel like a fool doing this but I started to wonder if maybe everything *was* my fault, as he constantly reminded me. There was no point in my asking where he had been when he did return; I wasn't going to get a satisfactory response anyway. So, I said nothing and descended into a state of complacency. This became the prevailing pattern whenever I expressed disapproval or made a request about anything. Walking on eggshells, afraid of causing a conflict, was exhausting. A few weeks later, after another similar incident, I told him that it had to end, and he had to move out.

"Look, this isn't working for me anymore. I don't really get any benefit from you living there. You make a mess of things, don't pay your half of the mortgage, and still come and go as you please. I can't live like this. It's too stressful. Enough is enough."

No sooner had I given him my edict (for the umpteenth time!) when he said, "But I want to marry you." I was stunned and just stood there with my mouth hanging open. For once in my life, I was totally speechless. He immediately embarked on the mission to convince me that I was being unreasonable, that a messed-up cupboard was no reason to end such a beautiful relationship, and that he would try to do better, after all we had the potential to have this beautiful life together now and in the future on his farm in Italy. I caved in because I so wanted to believe what he was saying was true. I didn't want to give up on the illusion of this fairy tale life with my wonderful prince even though I had become the bird in a gilded cage. I wanted to do the right thing because that was always the underlying motivation in almost everything I did. So, I chose to forgive him and put it all in the past, as I had done so many other times, and vowed that I would try not to be so critical, not keep tabs on him (even if he was gone overnight), and not complain about little things.

By 1993, I had the bright idea to bake bread for a living. It seemed to be the one thing that was missing from our little community. I got in touch with the owner of the only bakery in town and struck a deal with him to use his bakery at night. For the whole summer, I baked bread for the local farmer's market. It was a huge hit. The local newspaper wrote a big article about how I had transitioned from being a Hollywood producer to baking bread in a small Colorado town. Towards the end of the summer, one of my customers approached me and said he would like to finance a real bakery for me. Naturally, I was thrilled. The prince and I would be partners and the investor would be our silent partner. We spent all of September until mid-December building out the space and getting ready for the holiday season. All of my customers from the summer followed me to the bakery. Business was brisk and it seemed like success was inevitable.

December 24, 1993 - diary entry

It was going to be a very busy day at the bakery I opened one week ago. Word had gotten around about how good my sourdough bread was and business was picking up. We were rushing out the door at seven in the morning but it had snowed last night, and I hated driving in the snow. The prince grabbed the car keys and we headed out. I knew he was driving too fast for the road conditions, but I said nothing and just held on to the handle above the door. But the car skidded going around the curve and left the road, plummeting down the hillside, rolling twice before coming to rest right side up. We both jumped out of the car. The car was pretty much totaled. The back window was shattered, the roof was caved in, and there was significant damage to the sides. I just stood there, dumbfounded. I had bread to bake. I didn't have time for this! Neither of us had any bleeding injuries, so that was good. We were just ruffled up and in shock. Now we had to figure out how to get to the bakery!

"I have to report this to the police and the insurance company."

"Wait! Before you do that, I have a suggestion," the prince announced. He approached me, put his arms around my shoulders and whispered in my ear. I listened intently then pushed him away.

"I can't do *that*!"

"Who will know? It's a one-car accident, and no witnesses."

"But, but, but. . . why would I do this?"

"You first need to check your insurance policy and see if there are any restrictions and then decide. I know you will do the right thing. Then we will never speak of this again. It will be our little secret and I will deny any other story other than the one I gave you."

The prince said he would walk down to the main road and hitchhike to the bakery. He instructed me to go home and deal with the police and insurance company. I walked the two hundred meters back to the house and rummaged through a box of documents looking for my insurance policy on the car. As I flipped through page after page of conditions, I came to the rider that was attached. It's a good thing I was sitting down. There on the last page, at the very bottom, was the exclusion. I picked up the phone and set in motion the scenario that would dictate my life for the next six years.

It didn't take long for the investor to become a problem. The conditions of our agreement were that all the money he invested would have to be paid back in five years, and that included the salary he was paying his wife, who never once showed up to do anything. The agreement also stated that I would have to work for five years before I would own even one share of stock in a company I started from nothing. I was not happy about that and refused to sign the contract. Eventually things came to a head and the only recourse for me was to walk away and cut my losses.

A week or so later, a prominent business man approached the prince and offered to finance another restaurant. He wanted a high-end, sophisticated Italian menu, and was prepared to pay. The prince convinced me that I should come to work for him and make bread and pastries. I decided that it was a good challenge. We embarked on creating something out of nothing but it was more stress than I could ever have imagined but three months later the restaurant opened to rave reviews. However, our relationship took a toll. I worked in the restaurant in the morning until early afternoon. He showed up as I was leaving. If I tried to call him at home, he was never there, and the excuse was that he was out shopping, or doing something restaurant related. He almost always stayed until well after the restaurant closed at ten, and straggled home around midnight, or later. More often than not he came home drunk. We stopped having sex. Who had the energy anyway? A distance set in between us. I was so proud of all the work he had done to get this restaurant opened, and I worked as hard as I could to create bread and pastries that would make our customers happy. It should have been a joyous time, but there always seemed to be a lot of stress and strife. He wasn't even affectionate anymore and when he was it felt forced and was usually at my instigation.

One day I was in the pastry room mixing up a batch of bread when out of my mouth blurted, "Are you gay?"

"What? Why would you ask that?"

Why didn't he just say no?

"Why is it we don't have sex anymore?"

"What's the big deal? Haven't you had all the good sex you could want in your life?"

"Well, yes, I've had a lot of great sex, but I'm not *dead* yet!"

One or both of us was always annoyed with the other. It seemed to be on a trajectory of destruction, but we were tied together by the restaurant. The only thing to do was carry on. Then the investor demanded menu items that the prince refused to cook, and complained that our liquor costs were out of whack because both the prince and our general manager were helping themselves to the bar every day. One thing led to another and talks began for a buy-out of the prince's interest. According to the contract, he would be entitled to $50,000. Of course, it meant that when he left the restaurant, I also lost my job, but he told me not to worry because after all, he was going to have fifty-grand in cash. In October 1994, the buy-out ensued and he did indeed come home one day with a brown paper bag full of money and threw it on the bed where I was taking a nap. We laughed and had sex all over that fifty-grand, then it was bundled up in neat stacks and stashed in my underwear drawer. I never touched the money. He gave me five thousand as repayment for the preceding two years he lived with me and never contributed anything to the household. I was happy to have the money. With the stress of the restaurant out of our lives, things actually became harmonious. We were getting along really well, and I could see that he was putting in an effort to help around the house and be something other than a stressed-out grouch. I was back to believing in the fairy tale. We had entered into a glorious honeymoon period.

November 1994 – diary entry

It was a cold winter night and I was snuggled up in a chair next to the roaring fireplace. He pulled a stool up in front of me and sat down, leaning forward with a very intent look on his face as he studied me.

"I have a business proposition for you."

"Really?"

"Yes, and I think it's a good one."

"Okay, I'm listening. What is it?"

"We drive to Texas and pick up a kilo or two of cocaine and drive it back to Colorado." His eyes had a certain gleam that made my skin prickle.

"You're kidding, right?"

"Oh, no, I'm not kidding. You and I could be partners in crime."

I laughed. "I don't think so. That's the craziest thing I've ever heard. There are lots of miles between Texas and here and we could be stopped for a hundred reasons and going to jail at my age is not anything that's on my agenda. Not to mention the risk of having my property seized and a lot of other bad things."

He scowled. "So, you *won't* do it?"

"NO! And you shouldn't do it either. Get a job instead of looking to make illegal money that has so many risks."

He said nothing after that, but his eyes turned flat black. I had never seen anyone's eyes do that before. He got up, pushed the stool to the side, and stomped to his bedroom, slamming the door.

A week or ten days after that insane business proposal, I noticed that a good portion of the stacks of money was missing from the underwear drawer. Well, it *was* his money, and I had no right to question it. Later that day, I opened the freezer and saw a mysterious foil-wrapped package stashed in the back. I pulled it out and discovered much to my horror that it was a kilo of cocaine.

"That motherfucker!" I bellowed. "Who the hell does he think he is, Pablo Escobar?"

Then I panicked. I wanted to kill him. I wanted him out of my life before something really awful happened such as him being busted and the DEA seizing my assets. I was beside myself with rage. What was he doing behind my back? Dealing drugs obviously. This could not go on. When he walked in the door an hour later, I confronted him and told him to get both his cocaine and his sorry ass out of my house. He just looked at me, hung his head, a tear or two trickled down his cheek. He begged forgiveness, saying he had made a huge mistake but that he would abide by my wishes and remove the drugs. I never really knew what happened to them – until I started hearing hushed phone calls at odd hours of the day and night and found out later that he had been selling the cocaine in ounces but had been taking payments in the form of checks. Of course, all the checks bounced and he was out many thousands of dollars. By now, I was so stressed out I could hardly function. He made no attempt to move out. He simply stonewalled me, disappeared for a few days and waited until I calmed down and then started in with the hoovering and love-bombing. Besides selling the cocaine, he was also using. I could tell by the glassy look in his eyes and his clenched jaw. I had made it very clear to him that I had seen my share of drug abuse in the entertainment industry and I was not going to be a part of that culture again. He said he respected my wishes and was done with such activities. We were on rocky ground for sure. I told him, "I can't live like this; my life has always been well organized and as stress free as possible and all you have done with your erratic work history, little white lies, and now drug dealing, is to completely undo the life I had set up for myself. I can't take it anymore."

By now, we were barely talking, not sleeping together, and all the time I am wondering what the hell was I doing with this guy? Oh yeah, I almost forgot: the accident. After one final attempt to end it, he begged and pleaded for me to give him one final chance to prove he was worthy of my love and affection. I don't know what the hell possessed me to say okay.

The big problem was that he had spent the entire $50,000 and not paid the taxes on it. The IRS wasn't so happy and sent innumerable notices demanding twenty-grand in taxes, which of course, he didn't have. If there was one governmental agency I lived in fear of, it was the IRS. Other than that one year when he told me I could wait until the next year to file my taxes, I had always filed them on time. I started losing weight. I had anxiety through the roof. Whatever I ate went right through me. I had chest pains and was a bundle of nerves and started to wonder how long before I had a heart attack or stroke. We were locked in a dance of anger and deceit.

December 25, 1994 – diary entry

We arrived at our apartment hotel in Baja California at two in the afternoon. A friend of the prince picked us up at the airport and they insisted that we stop for a beer just on the other side of Cabo. I was still fuming about last night.

At three o'clock yesterday the prince told me he was taking his daughter out to dinner for Christmas Eve to a restaurant on the east side of Denver that they both liked a lot. I didn't have a problem with that and told him I hoped the two of them had a nice time. I also reminded him that we had an early morning flight to Cabo and he still had to pack. He assured me that he wouldn't be late. When he wasn't home by ten o'clock, I went to bed. I woke up at midnight, and he wasn't home then either. I started to worry. I tried to go back to sleep but tossed and turned. I must have dosed off lightly but I heard him open the front door. I looked at the clock on my nightstand. It was two o'clock.

"Where have you been?"

"I took my daughter to midnight mass."

"What?"

"I told you – we went to midnight mass."

There was something about the way he said it that made me not believe it. "We have to be up at four to leave at five for the airport," I reminded him, "and you haven't even packed yet."

"Oh, what the fuck is the big deal? I can pack in five minutes."

"I wish you would've called me. You told me you were just taking her to dinner when you left in the afternoon."

"Do you always have to be so controlling?"

"I don't think it's controlling to be worried when you are hours and hours late and we have a plane to catch."

I barely got another hour of sleep after that and the hour-long drive to the airport was tense. By the time we got to the airport, I wished I wasn't going on this trip. When we checked in at the airline counter and asked about seat assignments, I told the ticket agent, "I don't care where you seat me, just don't do it anywhere next to him!"

I wound up in row seven and he was seated at the back of the plane. I wasn't upset that he spent time with his daughter. I was upset that my gut told me he was lying about everything else, but of course without proof it just makes me sound paranoid and suspicious. As hard as it's going to be, I want to enjoy this time in Mexico after having worked all year and dealing with all the restaurant buy-out bullshit. I am going to enjoy myself no matter what.

Three days into the trip, everything seemed to be fine. He was being as sweet as he could be and I finally gave up being mad. We were at dinner a few nights later at his friend's restaurant when the friend mentioned that a local, whom he knew very well, had a small piece of land he wanted to sell. I asked the price and Enzo said it was around $4,000. I looked at the prince.

"What do you think? Should we at least look at it? You know my dream is to live in Mexico, and I do love it here."

He agreed, albeit reluctantly, and we went with two other people who were going to give us their honest opinion on whether it was a good lot to buy or not. The consensus was that it was a steal at that price. The next thing I knew I had written a check for $2,000 with the agreement that the other half – the prince's half – would be wire-transferred as soon as we got back to Colorado. We signed a purchase agreement and I was on cloud nine! My dream was going to come true.

July 1995 – diary entry

Today I was standing in the restaurant kitchen (yes, there was another restaurant!) about to leave for the day when the prince came in and started prepping for dinner. Our manager walked through the kitchen and saw us talking. He said, "When are you two getting married? I thought it was going to be this summer?"

"So did I, but you'll have to ask him," I said, pointing to the prince who was chopping and dicing onions and didn't even look up or acknowledge the manager's comment. When the manager walked back into the dining room, I said, "Now that Dieter mentioned it, *are* we going to get married?"

He put the knife down and looked up for the first time. "Sure, I'll marry you. I'll give you a title but you have to support me."

"Oh, yeah, right!" I scoffed, and walked to the rear of the kitchen to clock out. "That's pretty funny! You can't possibly be serious." When I passed through the kitchen on the way to the back door, he just stood there with the weirdest expression on his face. I couldn't tell what he was trying to convey. He didn't appear to be amused by my laughing at his comment. Was he serious about me supporting him? He couldn't possibly be. Then again. . . .

Fast forward to 1996: We had been together off and mostly on for nearly five years. We had set several wedding dates but never got past that point, although on two occasions I had actually either bought a dress or very expensive material to have one made. Something always came up that derailed the plans. Usually, it was because he got cold feet or said his daughter would never forgive him if he remarried. Then there was a cataclysmic event. His pre-pubescent daughter had threatened suicide. He was beside himself and was calling his sister in Italy begging her to please talk to her niece and his ex-wife and make sure that everything was okay. The sister had a better idea: She would come to Colorado and straighten things out. However, she had no money for a plane ticket, so he convinced me to pay for it with my TWA credit card and she made plans to come for about five weeks. She stayed with us and during that time engaged in various activities with his daughter, whom I barely knew, and his ex-wife. I was left at home, never included in anything. It was probably just as well.

One night as we were having dinner, the sister said, "I'm leaving soon and I don't want to leave until I see the two of you married."

The prince and I looked at one another and he said, "Well, I guess it's about time then. What do you think?"

"Okay. Let's do it!"

We hastily put together a small wedding with about twenty-five invitees. It was a crazy period because we had embarked on opening *yet another* restaurant and we had strict deadlines to meet if we were to open on time. Now we had one more circus trying to get everything together to get married.

A friend loaned me her ivory satin wedding dress and another friend offered her spacious house as a location. His sister made my veil but I had no time to buy proper shoes, so I wore my Tony Lama cowboy boots! My friend Anna would've laughed at that! The night before the wedding, we were sitting around the kitchen table as his sister polished my nails, and she asked, "Why hasn't he brought you to Italy to meet the family? You've been together five years now. That's plenty of time."

"We're planning on retiring on the farm in a few years and then I can meet everyone."

She stopped painting my nails and just stared at me.

"What farm?"

"The farm he owns outside Milan," I said cheerfully.

She just kept staring at me.

"There's no farm in Italy," she said soberly. "We lost that two decades ago."

I swiveled my head to the side and glared at him menacingly. The thought of canceling the wedding and still trying to open the restaurant made my head spin. I swallowed my anger and said nothing. What *could* I possibly say at this point? It took every ounce of control I had to keep from leaping across the table and strangling the life out of him.

The wedding ceremony was performed by a friend and it was actually a lovely affair. There was lots of champagne and a large selection of tasty *hors d'oeuvres*. Another friend gave us one night at the Marriott as a wedding present. I was feeling joyous and happy, swept along by the tide of emotion. The reception ended at eleven and we were both exhausted. We changed into casual clothes and headed for the Marriott. By the time we got to the hotel he seemed totally bored by the whole thing. I figured considering the revelation his sister made that he would make some attempt to smooth my feathers. But no. He crawled into bed, turned on the TV, and basically ignored me. I had to coerce him into having sex. He just wanted to go to sleep. The next morning, we had room service breakfast and then headed back to the mountains. The opening of the restaurant was the next day – Monday - and we still had a lot of details to attend to. But he was fixated on something else.

On the way home, he commented that it would be a good idea if he was a signatory on my checking account; that way he could pay the bills if for some reason I couldn't. That seemed reasonable enough; I had had joint accounts with two previous husbands without any problems, so I agreed. The next day we went to the bank and signed signature cards on our way to our new, jointly owned restaurant in Denver.

I immediately went into the kitchen and started preparing desserts for the evening's dinner crowd. He disappeared without saying a word. I had no idea where he'd gone but he strolled in four or five hours later sporting a new tattoo on his upper arm, covered in a large bandage. I was shocked.

"That must have been an expensive tattoo!"

"I didn't pay for it. I told the guy I would give him ten free pasta dinners at our restaurant in exchange."

There was something about the story that didn't add up. The next day I went to the tattoo parlor on the corner and wandered through the shop looking at various designs. The owner, a bearded biker with tatts from head to toe, asked me if I was looking for something specific. I smiled and told him that my husband had gotten a dragon tattoo the day before and I would really like to have a matching one, only a smaller version. He said, "Oh, yes, I remember."

"Do you think we could do a similar trade where you eat at our restaurant for free in exchange for doing the tattoo?" He just stared at me and said he had no idea what I was talking about. I told him what the prince had said and he said, "No, he paid the full amount." Now I had caught him in two big lies – the one about the farm and the one about the tattoo. (We won't even add in all the little white lies!) I didn't know what to do so as usual I did nothing. Said nothing. I was back to being in a holding pattern. It only took four days for the bounced check notices to start rolling in. He had written three different checks and all of them had bounced. He'd bought himself a $250 pair of sunglasses, a $140 tattoo, and there was a smaller check he had written to his ex-wife. I was furious. He'd certainly wasted no time taking advantage of being on my checking account. His prior experience with checking accounts should've been a warning.

The prince briefly had his own checking account at a small local bank. He'd made a modest deposit of several thousand dollars from the proceeds of the sale of the other restaurant. Within two or three weeks, we were getting phone calls from the bank saying he had to come in to sort out some paperwork. Since it was his account I merely passed along the messages and assumed that he had gone there and dealt with whatever the issues were. Less than a month later, a letter from the bank was in my post office box. I opened it. The content of the letter was short and sweet: "Please come to the bank and close out your account. We no longer wish to have you as a client." He went to the bank and withdrew the funds and when I asked what the problem had been, he blamed it on some SNAFU at the bank. Nothing was ever his fault.

Now, after catching him lying *again*, I was so furious that I told him I wanted the marriage annulled. I screamed at him that he had no business taking the checkbook out of my purse, writing checks, and not telling me he had done it, or worse yet, not writing them in the register. He never seemed to grasp the concept that in order to write checks, there should actually be money in the account to cover them. I was shaking with rage because now I had to figure out how to cover all those checks.

One of our customers at the restaurant that night was our business lawyer. After the crowd thinned out, I got him cornered. "I want you to file for an annulment."

He gasped, "You've only been married a week!" Then he promptly talked me out of it, citing a misunderstanding, a miscommunication, an adjustment period.

"You don't understand," I wailed. "This was the last straw; I have been deceived from the beginning and see no end in sight to this madness!" When he said I should give it another chance, I started sobbing. My head was spinning from trying to sort out what I should do. We were now business partners in a restaurant and it wasn't so easy to just walk away. I would live to regret that for the next twenty years.

Two months later, I went to the post office before work to find a notice from the IRS. They were attaching my (now joint) bank account, but thankfully, the levy was issued on the day before I made a deposit so all they got was a small fraction of what they were owed. What ensued after that was a nightmare beyond belief. We had to hire a lawyer, have the prince declared non-collectable, and then wait three years before he could file bankruptcy and discharge his tax liability. It was one thing after another and he left the task of managing all these disasters to me. During all of this, he had a falling out with the third partner in the restaurant and insisted that he buy both of us out and end our business relationship. The prince claimed he had caught the other partner stealing money from the cash receipts at the end of the night, but that wasn't something our very German partner was inclined to do. When I pressured the prince for the real reason he wanted out of the restaurant, he said it was because "the Kraut insulted you by saying you looked like a fifty-year-old woman" – which is what I was! Before I knew it we were all sitting in the lawyer's office signing papers and getting a small buy-out for our ownership percentage. What that really meant was that the prince had a small cushion to live on and therefore didn't need to work. I impressed upon him that the money would only last four or five months and he should consider looking for a job.

The defining moment (as if there needed to be another one) in this short, tumultuous marriage, came in July 1996, six months after we were married and about the time the buy-out from the restaurant was dwindling. One of his friends, a rather shady character I would learn later, told me about a new kind of mortgage that was available through the company he worked for and that I should consider refinancing my house, (on which I owed less than $40,000). He claimed this mortgage was risk free and with an adjustable rate I would be locked in for five years and when the mortgage re-set I could then refinance again. He said it was foolish to have so much equity that was doing nothing for me. I told him that my mother had always told me that one's home was sacrosanct and should never be encumbered in any way. He scoffed and told me that was "old thinking" and that I would be so much better off if I did what he was suggesting. The strongest argument for doing it came from the prince himself, who said he had just received a job offer in the Cayman Islands. He gave me quite the convincing argument about how I could bring some of the money there and invest it in a high yield account. Having worked in private banking in New York, I knew something about offshore accounts and this intrigued me, so I agreed to do it, and took out $40,000 in equity plus refinancing fees, paid off a small tax bill I had, and entertained the idea of enclosing the front porch to turn it into a sun room where I could grow orchids and move in a desk where I could have a writing space. The remainder of the money was going to the Caymans. Of course, not three days after I got the check than the job offer had "vaporized" and he was once again without any income. Now seemed like the most propitious time to embark on the sun room project so we made an agreement that I would pay all the bills for the household if he would enclose the porch. He agreed. But even after the month-long project was completed, he made no effort to find a job and I wound up paying all the bills out of my refi money for the next six months. I was starting to see a pattern here and it was causing me great distress. To put it bluntly, I was fed up. I had had enough of the whorl of lies and deceit, his inability to keep a job even when he had created it, and his constant friction with friends and partners. It was becoming pretty obvious that he was unstable.

One morning after breakfast, I initiated a conversation about his work plans, and within two minutes of what I thought was going to be a constructive discussion, he got up and stormed out of the house, and disappeared. What surprised me the most is that I was relieved. It was getting to the point where the only time I wasn't gripped by anxiety or fear was when he was gone.

Later that day, it was time for me to walk the dog. I usually walked him on the road in front of my house and up a steep hillside to an open meadow. As I climbed the hill, I heard the prince's voice resonating from a neighbor's house.

"The fucking bitch is driving me crazy. I don't know how much more I can take," he whined to our alcoholic, deadbeat neighbor.

"Well, you just make sure that you get part of her house before you go!"

"Don't worry. I plan to. I got her to refinance it and now I am on the paperwork."

My knees buckled and I dropped to the ground. Now it made sense why he pressured me so to do the refi on my house. Ending this marriage was not going to be easy because his goal was to get something, anything, out of me, and the only big asset I had was my house, which he now co-owned. I trudged up to the meadow and sat on top of a hill, cradling my head in my hands and sobbing. My world was swirling into an abyss and I knew one wrong move would cost me.

When I came back to the house, he was still gone. I don't remember what happened next, only that I felt the room start to spin. Before I could sit down on the sofa, my knees gave out and I slumped to the floor. The sound of the front door opening aroused me. I was still lying on my side. I didn't move. I decided I would wait until he said something or asked if I was okay, but instead he stepped over me as if I was a bag of trash and walked to the kitchen. What the hell was I going to do? I needed help. But I had no one to talk to. By now most of my friends had grown weary of listening to the constant litany of his bad behavior. Even Anna told me, "Sweetie, I don't know what's happened to you, but you need to straighten out your life. I'm here for you, but only you can know what to do about this mess you've gotten yourself into." Oh, great, my best friend was shutting me out and on reflection, it was with damn good reason. I had called her crying at least a dozen times, running every scenario by her, and all she would do was cluck in mock horror at the situations I described. Now I was completely isolated. I desperately needed to talk to someone who could help me sort this out. I made an appointment at the local mental health clinic and at my first session a few days later, I poured out my story of my relationship with the prince and how I was always in a state of high anxiety and fear.

"Fear of what?" she asked.

"I don't know. I just have a sense of impending doom as though any minute my life will explode."

"Why don't you just leave?" she asked, twirling her pen between her fingers.

"I can't leave. It's *my* house. Or it *was* my house. Now his name is on it."

"Have you thought about calling the sheriff to get him out of your house?"

"Yes, but I'm afraid to. I think that would make things worse."

"Has he ever hit you?"

"No, never. But he is quietly terrorizing me in my own home. I tiptoe around making sure to never say or do anything to set him off. Just when I think it can't get any worse, he turns into the person I fell in love with, which throws me off balance. Then we have these honeymoon periods, which are blissful. Now I'm just confused and scared. I can't think straight enough to come up with a way to extricate myself from this marriage without imperiling my finances and maybe even my life."

"You certainly have an untenable situation here but maybe by working together, we can find a solution that will liberate you and help you see things more clearly."

She made another appointment for the next week and asked me to bring a list of his good and bad traits and how I envisioned this working out to my advantage. To be honest, I didn't think I had an advantage.

I told him I had gone to see a therapist. He was less than pleased. The way he was stomping around the house told me all I needed to know – he was going to try and intimidate me into not going.

"You're not telling her about our personal lives, are you?" he asked as he slammed the refrigerator door. "What goes on between us is our business, not someone else's. I don't like that you're doing this at all. You need to keep our lives private!" he said over his shoulder as he stormed off to his bedroom and slammed the door. I canceled my appointment with the therapist.

Now we were barely speaking – a nod here, a grunt there, no eye contact. He was giving me the silent treatment, which is an extreme form of abuse. We were literal ships passing in the night and some days we didn't speak at all. I was walking on eggshells, wondering what he was going to do next. I wanted to be invisible. I wanted him to leave. It was as though I had some menacing stranger living in my house. I started locking my bedroom door at night. It pained me to do that, but I had had a nightmare that he sneaked into my bedroom and bashed my head in. I knew that was irrational, but I was gripped by terror of all the things I didn't know. He certainly wasn't the effusive, charming, erudite prince I had met six years ago. He was cold, distant, angry, and exuded a palpable negative energy that paralyzed me with anxiety and mind-altering fear. Who knew what he was capable of? This went on for several weeks until I was fast approaching a breaking point.

One night I'd forgotten to lock my bedroom door and sometime in the middle of the night he crawled into my bed and put his arms around me and apologized, telling me what a fool he'd been, how he was so very sorry, how I was the love of his life, and that he had learned his lesson.

"Really? What's the lesson you've learned from all of this?"

"I'm not really sure, but I learned it."

He was affectionate and loving and wore down my resolve and we had sex for the first time in weeks. But as usual he tossed and turned, snorted and grunted, and I was desperate for sleep so I disentangled myself and moved to the far edge of the bed. For the first time in many months, I thought that maybe this could all work out after all. I felt happy for the first time in ages but as I snuggled into the down comforter, ready to drift off to sleep, he pulled his knee back and thrust it hard against my hip.

"What the *fuck* did you just do to me?" I bellowed between sobs of pain.

"What? It was an accident."

There was no way that was an accident. I pushed him out of the bed and told him to go back to the other room. When I got out of bed in the morning, I could barely put weight on that leg and had trouble walking for three weeks afterwards. That was the last time we ever slept in the same bed for the rest of our twenty-year marriage.

On a daily basis, we loped along. Some days were okay, others not so much. He confessed that he acted out because I was so controlling and critical. I vowed that I would try to be less so if he would stop telling me white lies, being secretive about his whereabouts when he wasn't home, and stop screaming at me over things that were meaningless. We agreed to try and "work it out." This was the first time that I had any real hope that this relationship would go on. He actually seemed to be trying. We hadn't had an argument in weeks, he made an attempt to be pleasant, and we made a point of doing things together such as hiking up in the wilderness and having friends over for lunch on the deck. I had started to relax and tried as hard as I could to just let go of things from the past and only think of our future life together. It was a really blissful period. So determined was I to make this work that I destroyed everything I had written that was negative. I wanted only good things in my life and in our relationship.

By 1997, he had decided that the only job he was going to get was to create another restaurant.

"Partners were always the problem," he told me, "but if I *just* had a small hole-in-the-wall restaurant that you and I could run, we could generate enough income to give us a nice life. I found a good location, a tiny place in a popular district in Denver just one block away from the big health food store where all the yuppies shop. Let me take you there tomorrow and you can see for yourself. I think it would work perfectly." He looked at me adoringly and stared into my eyes as he said it.

He was on his best behavior when he took me to see the location. At this time, I, too, was out of work after the last restaurant debacle and the money left-over from the refi was dwindling fast.

"I don't have enough to finance this," I told him as we peered through the windows.

"Don't worry, I've already talked to a friend who said he would put up most of the money." It was the brother of the guy we stayed with in Aspen, I learned later. "But I still need to come up with ten-grand."

"Well, I *don't* have it," I replied emphatically.

He smiled, put his arm around me, and said, "Oh, but you *do*. In your house. And you should have *some* money lefover from the refi."

I stared at him disbelievingly. "You want me to put up my house as collateral? Uh, I don't think so."

"Not all of it, just ten-grand worth."

"NO! Absolutely not."

"Would you at least talk to the real estate agents? They will tell you why it's such a good deal for us."

"Maybe. I don't know. This is a lot to ask of me." *Especially after all the other shit you've put me through.*

The next day the real estate agent came to see me and told me that the financials on this little place looked good, that it was a moneymaker and it would be a shame that he couldn't open it because of a lousy ten grand when the other guy was putting up $35,000 for improvements, etc. Dorothy was giving me a good, old fashioned dose of Jewish guilt. And laying it on thick. I felt pressured. I didn't want to do it, but both the agent and the prince insisted it was a win-win for me – that I would have income once again and the promissory note for the ten thousand would only be about $240 a month and we would have no trouble generating that payment. I was shaking with both rage and indecision, but they both kept pounding me until I gave in. His coercive arguments were always laced with comments such as "I'm just trying to earn a living," or "you're my wife; you're supposed to help me." He made me feel as though by doing this good deed I was going to save both our lives.

One month later, the restaurant opened. Business was good because we kept many of the customers of the previous owner, but at the end of the day I could never balance the cash drawer. When I asked him about it, his response was "So I took twenty bucks, what's the big deal?" This was just a hint of what was coming.

I did my shift in the morning and went home at two o'clock. He arrived as I was getting ready to leave and was supposed to stay until it closed at nine, but sometimes I would call to see how business was doing and there would be no answer. I found out later that he would close up the restaurant and go to the bar across the street and drink with one of his buddies. I realized that disaster loomed and I was about to lose my ten-grand, plus the other seven or eight thousand left-over from the refi that went into setting up the restaurant, paying for permits and licenses, and paying for someone to help with readying it for opening, *plus* I would have a lien on my house with no way to pay it off. Failure was on the horizon. And it did indeed fail. In a total panic I called therapist at the local mental health clinic and begged for an emergency session.

"I am so gripped with fear and anxiety I can't think straight," I sobbed. "I can't believe I fell for his bullshit – not only is he on the deed to my house, but I now have a lien on it, and I'm tied into a restaurant deal with him that is on the brink of utter failure. I'm completely freaking out and bouncing off the walls trying to sort this mess. I feel as though I am mired in quicksand, with no way to get out." I sat there crying and twirling a strand of my hair.

"Clearly you are in a state of distress," she acknowledged, "but I have something that will help you stay calm until you can sort out your marriage and business dealings with this man." She made another appointment for the next day.

I reluctantly accepted the sample box of the antidepressant, walked out to my car and tore open the package, and dry swallowed a pill. It only took a couple of days for the antidepressant to have a very bad effect on me and I spiraled out of control. I refused to go to the restaurant but he went there anyway, even though it was on the verge of closing. Several days later, after another session with the shrink, when it finally dawned on me how fucked-over I was, I called him at the restaurant and told him I couldn't take another day of this turmoil, that I might as well drive my car off a mountaintop because I didn't see any way out of the mess he had created. I was having a full-blown panic attack. Imagine my surprise when a police car and an ambulance showed up in my driveway. The cops were polite when I opened the door.

"Ma'am, your husband called us and said you were suicidal. He instructed us to take you to a local hospital for evaluation."

"What? I'm *not* suicidal. I was *upset*, nothing more. We'd just had an argument. It wasn't anything so serious as to require my going to a hospital!"

"Well, that's not what your husband told us. He indicated to the dispatcher that you were clearly suicidal and that we needed to take you in," he said, thumbs tucked into his belt and rocking back and forth on his heels. "So, get your purse or whatever you need, the ambulance is waiting. You can go peacefully, or we can do it another way. It's your choice."

What the fuck had he done *now*? The ambulance first took me to a local emergency room where they stashed me in a little cubicle to wait for the intake doctor. I explained what happened, that I had just been very stressed out and didn't think the antidepressant I was given was helping at all.

"Well, those issues can be addressed during your stay at the local psychiatric hospital. They will adjust your medication or perhaps add another one. You can get dressed now; the ambulance will take you there."

There I was, locked up for the traditional seventy-two hour hold all because I was so distraught that he had hosed his friend for a total of forty grand, conned the ten thousand plus out of me, and then just closed up the restaurant and walked away as if nothing had happened. He hadn't invested one cent, so what did it matter to him? The most troubling realization came when I saw how much power he had over me if he could have me locked up in a psych ward just on his word.

To say this was a hellish experience would be the understatement of the century. There I was sharing a room with a young woman who had tried to commit suicide by slashing her throat, all because she decided that Jesus didn't love her. Then there were the people who screamed and pounded nonstop on the walls of their padded cell, or paced up and down the hallway from the side effects of the drugs they were on. Most of them were doing the Thorazine Shuffle, just as they did in *One Flew Over the Cuckoo's Nest*. One of the scariest characters was a Native American woman with bright, neon orange lipstick smeared at least a half-inch outside her lip line who sat in a corner all day mumbling to herself and peeing on the floor. It was like something out of a Fellini movie.

During the one hour that we were allowed telephone calls, I called the prince and hissed into the phone, "You listen to me, you little shit; you better figure out how the fuck to get me out of here otherwise when I *do* get out, you're going to regret having called the police on me!"

I couldn't believe that I was in such a place and that *he* had put me here. I was actually terrified of some of the other patients so I didn't interact with any of them. This was not a place for me to cultivate friendships! Out of the corner of my eye, I saw the floor nurse making notes as I sat in a corner by myself. The only time I interacted with anyone was when it was mealtime and I shuffled to the cafeteria with the other inmates. The food was unpalatable. I fed my dog better food. I picked at it, but mostly I moved it around the metal tray. The only thing that was remotely edible was the tapioca pudding. By day two, I had had enough and went to the nurses' station and put on my best smile and friendly demeanor.

"Do you think it's possible that I could meet with the nutritionist of this place? I'd like to talk to that person about the meals."

The head nurse pushed her glasses to the top of her head, looked at me quizzically, and asked, "Do you have special dietary needs or an allergy?"

"Yes! I have *both* of those things!"

"Well, you just have a seat in the waiting area against the wall and I will see if the dietitian is still on the premises."

Ten minutes later, a dowdy looking woman stood in front of me. She didn't look very happy. "Are you the patient who needed a consult about food restrictions?"

Finally, a bright spot in my day! "Yes, that would be *me*!" I said cheerfully.

"Come this way," she said, and led me to a small office just on the other side of the nurses' station. "So, what seems to be the problem with the food, and what foods are you allergic to?"

"I'm allergic to *all* of it! That isn't *food*! It's slop! I don't know what the hell that was on my plate today – something brown, I'm guessing some kind of meat – and what *might* have been creamed corn, I'm not sure."

"Are you allergic to meat and corn?"

"You *could* say that. I'm primarily a vegetarian so I don't eat meat and I don't generally eat food that isn't easily recognizable. Could you please order some salmon? I would like it grilled with just a bit of dill and lemon, please. And for vegetables, I would prefer *haricots verts*."

"Harry go *where*?" she asked, looking totally puzzled and holding the pen over her tablet waiting to write something down.

"*Haricots verts*! French green beans. That's what I want. You don't seem to understand that I only eat real food, and none of what was served to me in the past forty-eight hours falls into that category." I sat back with my arms folded across my chest. There! I told *her*! Did she not know that I was married to a famous chef and that our previous restaurants had won awards? That I was accustomed to eating only the best food available?

She made a few notes on her pad, then looked up over her wire-rimmed glasses, and said, "I'll see what I can do."

A sense of relief washed over me. At least I would get something decent to eat that night for dinner. While everyone else was served some kind of stew, a male nurse called my name and asked me to raise my hand. When I did, he approached my table and handed me my specially prepared dinner. I was so excited because by now I was starving! But what was *that* on the tray? I have no fucking idea. Something white, must have been fish, and what most certainly were canned green beans that were not green at all but a cross between yellow and brown. Thank God, there was the ever-present plastic cup of tapioca pudding.

The only thing worse than the food was the coffee. On a table near the nurses' station was a big urn where we could help ourselves. It tasted like burnt water. I went to the nurses' station and said, "Um, this stuff tastes awful," pointing to the Styrofoam cup. "Is there any way I could get a cappuccino? Pleeeeease?" I mean, seriously, where the hell did I think I was, The Golden Door?

She just stared at me then went back to making notes. "Oh, no, I'm sorry, caffeine isn't allowed. It might make the patients hyper."

I looked her blankly. "You've got these people doped on uppers, downers, and drugs that make you go sideways, and you're worried about a little caffeine?"

"Yes, frankly, we *are*. Now please go sit down and enjoy your *decaf*."

As soon as the seventy-two-hour hold was up, the prince arrived and insisted that this had all been a big mistake and that he knew I wasn't *really* suicidal, I had just been under a lot of stress. One of the conditions of my release was that I agreed to continue to see the therapist. I would've agreed to damn near anything to get out of *that* place. I grabbed what few things I had brought with me and we bolted for the door. I was so happy to see the "outside" that I had totally forgotten that *he* had put me there!

I went to see the therapist a few days after my release. I heard myself telling her over and over again, "I have to get out of this marriage."

"Why exactly did you marry him, if you already had indications that he was deceitful and manipulative?"

"I don't know," I moaned. "Pressure from his sister, for starters, and the fact that I didn't want to think the previous five years had all been a mistake. Also, he was so good at convincing me that things would be better and that I had simply over-reacted. And last but not least, I wanted to believe in *love*. I wanted to believe that we would be together forever and that I could always depend on him. It sounded so romantic to think this was the person I would spend the rest of my life with; that I wouldn't grow old alone; that he would always be there for me. I know that sounds stupid, but nonetheless, here I am. In a big fucking mess. Not knowing how to change anything."

The therapist was emphatic that we either had to work this out or I would have to end the relationship no matter what the cost. Was she kidding? I wasn't going to give him half my house. The only other recourse was to convince him to come to the therapist with me and to try and sort out our issues. He reluctantly agreed to accompany me to the next appointment the following week.

Well, that turned out to be a total waste of time. He sat in the chair and wouldn't say a word. The look on his face spoke volumes. He was pissed off and was not going to cooperate, so I spilled my guts, cried a bit, pleaded with him to at least air his grievances so I could make things better, but he stonewalled both me and the therapist. Clearly, this was not a solution. We left her office, me in tears, him mad as a bear, and driving erratically all the way home. I went to my bedroom, closed and locked the door, and lay on the bed wondering what the hell I was going to do now.

Scribbled on a yellowed, tear-stained index card in a nearly illegible scrawl

Every time I ask him to clarify something, he said that makes no sense at all, he screams at the top of his lungs, 'What? Am I speaking Chinese?' Then he storms off to his bedroom or flies out the door and disappears. Been going on like this for the last five years. Now February 1998.

August 1998

Last month, I was reading the celebrity news in New York City, and what did I see? An announcement about my old friend Catherine's new book and how she'd gotten a million-dollar advance! I was so happy for her. I went to her website and found her email address and sent her a congratulatory note. That set off a flurry of emails because we had not had any contact since I left New York nine years ago and moved back to the West Coast, and we had a lot of catching up to do. We were sending emails back and forth sometimes ten times a day catching up on our lives, loves, and other raucous adventures. I told her all about the prince, his good points and his bad points, and then I went into great detail about the circumstances that landed me in a State-run psychiatric hospital for seventy-two hours. Her next email said, "Oh my *God*! That is the *funniest* thing I have ever read. With all the other incidents with rock stars from your previous life, and *this,* you've got some fantastic material. Why aren't you writing about this stuff?"

"I just haven't had any focus or time to do that, because staying one step ahead of what the prince is plotting has been my full-time job!"

"Well, girlie, I am coming out to see you and you and I are going to write a screenplay. This is just too good to ignore. I'll get back to you later today with flight arrival info. Can't wait to see you! We are going to crank out a masterpiece based on your life! Mwa! Mwa!"

Ten days later she showed up. I picked her up at the airport and all the way home we chatted about everything and everybody in the last ten years. I gave her my bedroom and I slept in the sun room on the futon. Catherine was one of the most dynamic and entertaining women I had ever known. She was well educated, well-traveled, knew all the right people and a lot of wrong ones, too. She traveled in celeb circles gathering info to write about. I thought the prince would be excited to have such a famous person staying with us and with whom I was going to write a screenplay. *Au contraire.* He was sullen and moody and radiated annoyance from every pore. We all got up early, had coffee, sat on the deck and enjoyed the crisp mountain air – especially Catherine who still lived right in the middle of Manhattan. Then we plotted what we were going to write, made some structural notes, gobbled down some breakfast, and got to work. The prince quietly left the house about then and didn't show up until it was time to eat dinner. I have no idea where he went. He didn't have a job, but I was too engrossed in what I was doing to monitor his activities. He said he wanted to leave us in peace so we could write. But when he was here, he still had a scowl etched on his face, and wasn't really talking to either one of us. To say that this created tension would be a gross understatement, but I just ignored him. Catherine and I wrote ten hours or more a day. We laughed so hard about all the incidents we came up with that we incorporated into the plot, and gave special treatment to my dialogue with the nutritionist about those "Harry go where" things I wanted for dinner. By the end of ten days, we had gotten the entire script done and Catherine was off to NYC to deliver it to her agent.

When I got home from taking her to the airport, the prince was sitting on the deck drinking a beer. He still had the scowl and the look of displeasure on his face.

"Now life can go back to normal!" I said, as a prelude to my expressing how disappointed I was that he wasn't nicer to her or more sociable during her visit.

"I figured you girls needed space so I just disappeared to give you that. Was there a problem?"

"Only that you weren't very talkative or even very welcoming to one of my oldest friends. In fact, if I were to be brutally honest, you were downright rude. And I actually thought that maybe you would've offered to fix us dinner every night because we were working so hard during the day. But instead, I still had to go food shopping and cook for all of us when I should've been working. But never mind. She's gone and now we just have to wait to see what kind of response we get from her agent."

Without saying a word, he got up and went into the house and threw the beer bottle in the trash before retreating to his bedroom and closing the door. I followed him and knocked twice on the door before opening it.

"I don't know why you are always in a snit. It doesn't seem that you are very happy living with me. At least that's how it appears when you act like this."

"I'm just sick of being your punching bag."

"What the hell does *that* mean?

"No matter what I do it's never enough or good enough for you. All you do is criticize me."

"Well, that's just not true. The things I complain about are things that shouldn't be done in a relationship – such as lying, disappearing, insulting me, calling me names, treating my house as if it's a hotel, giving me the silent treatment for days and sometimes weeks on end. Are you telling me I shouldn't object to those things?"

"I don't think I'm *that* bad. And you're Miss Perfect? I don't think so," he said smugly. "After all, you've been married five times."

"That's not true and you know it. It was only twice before, and besides we aren't talking about *me*! We're talking about your behavior and how it affects our lives."

"You're making a big deal out of nothing. I need to take a nap. Please close the door."

"Just so we're clear here – the way you treat me, the names you call me, and the way you disrespect me, well, one day I'm going to stop loving you."

"Close the door and leave me alone!"

Well! That was a constructive conversation. Just like all the others.

January 1999 – diary entry

Today was my hearing before the administrative judge for Social Security. The judge would be the ultimate arbiter of whether or not my claim for disability was valid. After having shoulder surgery last month (I had in fact injured my shoulder in that rollover accident in 1993) and was looking at months of rehab, plus I was still suffering from PTSD, which the therapist I had been seeing attributed to the emotional abuse he had inflicted on me.

The decision was finally rendered in September 1999. It was twenty-seven pages long and detailed everything about my condition since 1997. The judge ruled in my favor stating that my PTSD was so severe and prolonged that it was unlikely that I would ever recover at all and therefore I was entitled to disability. Specifically, she stated that my records indicated that I was not suffering from any type of mental illness, that I was healthy other than having had extensive surgery on my shoulder, but she concluded that I was so severely traumatized by the events in my life that I would never again be employable. Well, what the fuck?

July 1999 – diary entry

There's a guy on one of the chat rooms I belong to who's been emailing me. We've struck up a friendship, discovered we have a lot in common, and share a similar sense of humor. Most of the emails are about the topic of the chat room, but eventually we moved into more personal areas and I found out he lived just outside Colorado Springs, was a well-known artist, well educated, and seemingly very enlightened. After many months of superficial exchanges, we got down to more serious matters – life, love, relationships, marriage, divorce, and all the agony that comes with each of those things. In a moment of weakness, I confided about my rocky marriage to the prince. Ted listened and responded with encouraging words, most important of which were "I am here if you ever need anything." I really needed to hear that, and I also need his friendship desperately because I have wound up swimming in this pond all by myself with no lifeline to the shore. Some days I think I am going to drown in confusion and turmoil. Ted and I emailed each other almost every day and when I was home alone or very late at night, we would talk for hours on the phone. He made me feel safe and cared for.

November 1999 – diary entry

Ted and I are talking on a regular basis now. I don't know how many times I have broken down and cried about how unhappy and afraid I am of staying in this marriage to the prince. Ted suggested that I pack a bag, grab the dog, and come down to his farmhouse and chill out until I can figure out what to do. I told him I was grateful for that offer, but because it was *my* house, it wasn't going to be in my best interest to leave, but rather that I had to get my husband out of there. Ted gave me the strength and encouragement I needed to think about how I was going to do this instead of always being in a spin cycle and never being able to form a cogent plan or even a well-constructed thought. I felt as though he was my guardian angel. I told no one about our relationship; there was nothing to tell. It was totally innocent but it was also very intense on a lot of different levels.

Since the prince went to bed very early – seven o'clock or even earlier on some nights, I would call Teddy and sit in the sun room with the door to the living room closed. There was no heat in the sun room so I would have to put on my polar fleece and a pair of gloves to be able to sit there for two hours while we talked on the phone. I told Teddy I was going to ask for a divorce. I wasn't sure at what point I was going to do this, but the reality was that life with this guy was becoming increasingly more stressful and dangerous. I lived in constant fear, of what I wasn't even sure, but my gut told me that I was always in a state of danger and should pretty much expect the unexpected. There were some nights when I wish Ted was there to put his arms around me and tell me that everything was going to be okay. He was the only person in whom I had confided about the shit storm that was my marriage to someone I didn't know and didn't understand anymore. One night I was so distressed that he offered to meet me halfway – someplace in Denver – where we could sit and talk. I told him that was impossible. I didn't want to create any situation that I would have to explain and I would certainly have some 'splainin' to do if the prince got up and discovered me gone. I needed to wait. There could be no slip-ups and nothing that smacked of impropriety on my part.

By now, my life had been reduced to five failed restaurant projects, two bankruptcies, the repossession of our car, and a constant struggle to stay one step ahead of this one-person destruction derby to whom I was married.

December 20, 1999 – diary entry

On the evening of December 17, when he staggered in many hours late and drunk, I was furious. "The least you could do is call me and tell me you're running late. Look outside. It's snowing. The roads are icy. The entire mountain community is on accident alert. I-70 is a mess. Anything could've happened between there and here."

"What the fuck do you want from me?" he bellowed.

"What do I want? Okay, I'll tell ya what I *want*. I want a goddamn divorce! I am sick of you and your lies and your hidden agendas and your abuse and lack of respect for me. This is over. I am DONE! Monday I am going to the courthouse and getting the papers."

"Fucking bitch," he growled, "I'm just your punching bag," and stormed off to the bedroom and slammed the door.

Considering he was drunk, I knew he would soon be asleep and snoring like a goat. I stood outside his bedroom door and listened. When I heard the familiar snorts and grunts, I knew he was out cold. I put on my polar fleece and plugged the little heater in out in the sun room and waited for the room to warm up a few degrees above freezing. Then I called Teddy.

"Hello, gorgeous," he said when he answered the phone.

"How'd you know it was me?"

"Your number came up on caller ID. What's up?"

"I did it! I finally did IT!"

"Did what?"

"Told him I wanted a divorce. That I was done with all the bullshit and that Monday I was going to get the papers and put an end to this nightmare."

"Well, that's *something*. How do you feel now?"

"I feel relieved. There isn't any way to fix what's wrong in this relationship. I could change the way I do everything, never complain, never confront him when I catch him lying, never ask for an explanation to the things that make no sense.

It just wouldn't matter. At this point we've been married under four years. I can recover from this."

Most importantly, the statute of limitations on the 1993 accident would run in five days.

"I must say that I am extremely proud of you. What finally made you do it?"

"He came home drunk, yet again. He'd told me in the morning that he would definitely be home in time for dinner, which is almost always around five. At eight o'clock he strolled in like nothing was wrong and when I pointed out that the least he could've done was called me so I wouldn't worry – I mean, good God, there's a snowstorm out there now – he said his usual line, 'What the fuck do you want from me?' That was my opening! I told him I wanted a goddamn divorce!"

"Are you okay? You seem very calm, considering that must have been quite a tumultuous and upsetting exchange."

"Yes, I'm fine. Well, as fine as I could be under the circumstances. I also bit off a piece of Xanax just to stop the world from spinning out of control."

"Can I do anything for you?"

"Aw, Teddy. You've been such a good friend to me the last year. I am really grateful to you for all your support and friendship."

"It's not anything you need to thank me for. I care about you tremendously, and just want you to be happy so you can continue writing and pursuing your dreams."

"It would be nice for this nightmare to end first and then I can think about dreaming."

We talked for another half hour before it was just too cold for me to sit there. We said our goodbyes and I turned on the TV to watch the ten o'clock news. I had the volume turned down as low as I could get it and still hear what they were saying. But from the back bedroom came his typical grumbling when I was making too much noise, so I shut off the television and tiptoed to my bedroom rather than risk him coming out and terrorizing me. At this point, I was in a zombie state. I knew I should feel something but I wasn't sure what that was.

The next day he was going to visit a potential tile job with a friend. I was relieved to have the day to myself and finally felt at peace at having made the decision to end it once and for all. I went about my errands and came home around three o'clock to see the answering machine blinking. It was his friend Gary, who had been the driver of the car. He said they had had an accident and that the prince had been flown in a flight-for-life helicopter to the local trauma center and that was where he was calling from. As I was listening to the message, my hands began to shake. NO! This can*not* be happening. Then the phone rang. It was Gary. After he told me about the accident, I asked, "Was the son of a bitch wearing his seat belt?" Of course, he wasn't because he hated wearing a seat belt and rarely ever did. The law didn't matter one whit to him. Laws were not for people with his aristocratic heritage, he told me once. Gary said I had to go to St. Martin's to pick him up. Oh, for fuck sake!

I had just walked in the door with bags of groceries so I needed to put everything away first. Then I had to collect my thoughts and figure out how I was going to deal with this. It was a thirty-minute drive to the hospital. I would try to get my head under control before I got there. When I walked into the ER there he was, propped up in a hospital bed, with IVs, a catheter, and his clothes cut off him.

"What the fuck have you done *now*?" I said between my clenched jaw. My instinct was to go bat shit crazy but I took a deep breath and stood there, staring at him.

Just then the ER doctor came in and asked to talk to me in the hallway. He told me the prince suffered a traumatic brain injury; that he 'might' make a full recovery in two or three years, but it would take lots of treatment and probably different medications. "There's not much we can do for him here, so the best thing is for him to be at home where it's quiet. Here is a list of signs you should watch out for and if he develops any of these symptoms, bring him right back here. Otherwise, the best thing is for you to get him to a neurologist and develop a treatment plan. . . ." Whatever the ER doc told me after that wafted around my head like a distant echo. My mind was spinning and suddenly my knees turned to jelly. I put my hand against the wall to steady myself. Just as I was about to crumple to the floor, the doctor led me to a chair so I could sit down. He thought I was upset about the accident, which of course I was, but not for the reasons he thought. I was completely unnerved because any hope I had of getting away from him was completely dashed at this point.

After we got home from the emergency room, I was beside myself. How was this going to play out now? Last night I told him I wanted a divorce and now here he was with a traumatic brain injury, which the doctor told me was going to be a long and difficult recovery and that I would need patience and understanding. I can't blame the doctor for not knowing that I had run out of both of those things, and all I really wanted now was to be free of this proverbial albatross around my neck.

The prince went to bed around seven o'clock. The ER had sent him home with some meds that were designed to knock him out. I waited until I heard him snoring and then I called Teddy.

"I'm going to put my head in the oven," I whimpered.

"Sweetheart, what's wrong?"

I started crying. Between sobs I told him about the accident, how he had a brain injury; that he might recover – in two or three years – and that my life was now officially ruined. "I don't know if I can do this."

"Why do you have to do anything?" he asked, in a concerned voice.

"What am I supposed to do? If I file for divorce, he will have to move out of my house, but he's not going to be able to work, so who's going to pay for his living expenses? Not me, surely, but that's what I am afraid will happen. You know how I felt about my commitment to marriage: I didn't want another divorce, I took those vows seriously – in sickness and in health – till death do us part – but he just made my life so miserable with all his bad behavior that I can't take it anymore."

"I understand what you're saying. But he has family. Maybe the best thing to do is ask his sister or his daughter to come to his aid. Considering everything, you shouldn't feel obligated to care for him."

"I know," I sighed, "but I do. Not because I care about him or even still love him, but what would it say about *me* if I abandoned him now?"

"I think it would say you did the best you could and he had an unfortunate accident that wasn't your fault and you have no more responsibility for him. But, I think it would be wise to examine exactly *why* you feel obligated to do this after all he's done to you. Is it because you want to do a good deed? Do you feel bound by the vows you took even though you suspect he didn't honor them? Or are you simply afraid of what people will think of you for leaving him?"

My head felt as though it was going to explode. I knew Teddy was right. This wasn't on me, but then again it was. I could barely stop crying long enough to even get a sentence out.

"It's complicated, and there is no easy or even right answer that I can give you. It is probably a combination of all of those things. I just want to do the right thing, but I don't even know what that is anymore."

"Look, I'm getting in my car right now, and I am driving towards Denver. Do you think you could meet me down on Simms? I can be there in an hour."

"I can't. It's snowing like hell up here and the plow won't come until morning, so even if I could get out now, I wouldn't be able to get home. And then what? If I have a mess now, that would make things even worse. But thank you. I really appreciate that you would do that for me."

"Honey, you don't deserve this at all. I just want to give you a big hug and let you know that everything is going to be okay. I am here anytime you want to talk. If you need someplace to escape to, come to my house – this big ol' farmhouse is too big for one person anyway. I have an entire wing that you could have all to yourself. I just want you to know that's an option should you need to flee – doesn't matter what time of the day or night. You hear me?"

"Yes," I said softly. "You're the best. Thank you."

January 20 – diary entry

He filed a lawsuit against the driver of the car. Of course, to bolster his claim that he had been irreparably damaged in the accident, there were dozens of doctors, IMEs, medication, tests, evaluations, therapy, both physical and speech, and on and on and on. Then came the disability claims and more doctor appointments, and bullshit sessions with psychiatrists, psychologists, and a neurologist, and at each appointment he made a stellar performance of being incapacitated. There were also two separate incidents where he was confined to the neuropsychiatric ward of a brain injury rehab hospital for three weeks each time. As the second hospitalization was coming to an end, the thought crossed my mind to just leave him there. I didn't want this responsibility after all he had put me through so I sent emails to several of his family members but none of them were willing to have him come live with them. Especially now! I was stuck.

February 2000 – diary entry

He's decided that now was the time to file bankruptcy for this mountain of restaurant debt and his debt to the IRS. I scrambled for weeks getting the paperwork together and trying to find a lawyer we could afford to do the bankruptcy. It was a nightmare. I couldn't eat, I couldn't sleep. There was only one person I could go to and that was the therapist at the mental health clinic who told me three years ago in no uncertain terms to get away from him as soon as possible; that I had PTSD from the systematic abuse he had been heaping on me since the very beginning of our relationship. At that time, I had never heard of PTSD, other than as it applied to war vets, so I went to the library and checked out a half dozen books on the topic. I had every symptom. I was in a fog. My brain didn't work. I couldn't think straight, and I was still suffering from the effects of the antidepressant. I felt hopeless and desperate. I had flashbacks and nightmares and a sense of impending doom. I had heightened startle responses, but somehow, I carried on. Emotionally, I was numb. Totally dead inside. I felt as though I was in some kind of prison camp from which I could not escape. And despite his numerous threats to leave, he stayed put. The therapist even suggested that I was suffering from Stockholm Syndrome. You know, like Patty Hearst. When I thought about it, she was right. I was basically a hostage in a marriage that probably should never have taken place.

December 2001 – notes scribbled on a torn piece of paper

Hands shaking; can hardly write. Heart pounding, tears falling on the paper. My mother has been dead seven weeks. I've been home two weeks and barely recovered from the trauma of watching her die from metastatic breast cancer.

Feeling sad and restless so I baked an apple tart. It's snowing outside. The prince went to bed at six. Took the tart out of the oven and while it was cooling, I needed to make the *nappage*. I had stashed a jar of apricot jam in the back of the fridge. It needed to be melted down, thinned with some lemon juice, and strained to form a clear glaze. I opened the jar and it was completely empty. He had eaten all of it. The last straw. Burst into tears, standing at the kitchen sink, bent over, sobbing into my hands. Heard him fling open his bedroom door. Stormed into the kitchen and bellowed at the top of his lungs: "WHAT THE FUCK ARE YOUR CRYING ABOUT?"

"I miss my mom," I said softly, knowing better than to even mention the empty jam jar.

"WELL, I'M TRYING TO SLEEP!" Stomped down the hallway and slammed the door to his bedroom. Hear him muttering something unintelligible. Go to sofa and cry into a pillow. Terrified of him coming out of his room again. Urge to run. Can't take more. Grabbed my car keys and walked outside. Still snowing. Road not plowed. Too dangerous. Stood there watching the snow fall. Feel lost and alone, and very afraid.

January 2002

In 1993, the prince and I were having a discussion about the cases in Switzerland that involved returning stolen art and money to the Jews from whom those things had been confiscated. He told me he had a great idea that I should write about and that was the Nazi propaganda art that was stored in Pueblo, Colorado for the last fifty years. It was certainly an interesting topic so I went to the library and did a microfiche search for any articles that talked about this art and came up with a full page spread in *The Denver Post* that told the story of how it wound up there and how most of the pieces had been returned to Germany under Ronald Reagan.

The pieces extolling and celebrating the Nazis were held back and were housed in a small Army museum in Washington, D.C. One night over dinner, we were talking about this topic and how I could work it into a plot. Basically, it would be about some neo-Nazi trying to steal those pieces. When I asked him how it was that he became aware of these paintings, he got that strange look in his eyes and had a demonic grin. "Someone asked me to steal them!" I laughed, thinking that was more strange than funny.

Over the next few years, I did copious amounts of research and started writing a book. I sent samples of my work to several agents and found someone to represent me. By 2001, the manuscript was finished, and edited, but because of 9/11, everything had slowed down and that included the publishing business. My agent suggested going the self-published route for the time being while we continued to look for a home with a publisher. The prince had done a bathroom tile job for a wealthy client so he had some extra cash and offered to give me the money to pay for the publishing. I thought that was very sweet of him, so I proceeded with the process. In December, I received my box of books and marketing materials and proceeded to formulate a publicity campaign. For the first month, sales were brisk and I was very happy, especially when I received my first royalty check of several hundred dollars. When I showed the check to the prince, he was delighted. I thought he might actually be happy for me, but I soon found out he had another agenda. As I sat at my computer in the sun room writing emails to my friends telling them that I got my first royalty check, I heard him come up behind me. I swiveled around in my chair and he was standing there grinning from ear to ear.

"You look awfully happy right now. What's up?"

He shifted his weight and let out a little chuckle before saying, "Just think, for the rest of my life I get to live off half your book royalties."

That sent shivers up my spine. I knew then that when he gave me the money to do this, he had an agenda and it was not to help me succeed, but rather to secure future income for himself. At that point, I was paralyzed with indecision, but when I went to bed that night, I knew what I had to do: I stopped all publicity, canceled any scheduled book signings, and basically let the book sit there on Amazon. I no longer cared if I ever sold another book knowing that he was only interested in getting half of what I made on it. What a shame that was. The book got good reviews and had tremendous potential, but I was not going to let him benefit from all my hard work. The real kicker came many years later – twenty-five to be exact – then I figured out *why* someone would ask him to steal artwork.

February 2002

He was so convinced that he was going to wind up with hundreds of thousands of dollars, but after a two- week trial, the jury ruled against him and he got not one dime for his claimed injuries because he was not wearing his seat belt. What we did wind up with though was $180,000 worth of lawyers' fees that there was no way I was going to pay, so I filed bankruptcy. While I was putting together his medical records, I came across a report from an independent psychiatrist who was paid to evaluate the extent of his brain injury. The first couple of pages were background information but on the third page was a paragraph that stuck out like a blinking neon sign. It read: "Patient's complaints are inconsistent with a brain injury. It is my opinion that he is suffering from various psychiatric problems, including a thought disorder, which have probably existed since he was a teenager." So it wasn't just me who thought he was embellishing his injury. This doctor thought he was bullshitting, too. But he continued to seek treatment from a variety of medical professionals to substantiate why he couldn't work or earn a living. I was stuck with this burden with no way to get rid of him without him claiming that he couldn't work, couldn't live on the tiny Social Security disability payment, and that I would have to support him. I was in a perpetual spin cycle with no end in sight. I solicited help from his family but neither his sister, nor his nephews, had any interest in having this person live with them or even near them. His sister told me in no uncertain terms, "He will ruin my life if he lives with me." But it was perfectly okay if he ruined *my* life?

(What I learned from other victims of narcissistic abuse is that the narcissist will fake brain injuries, cancer, mental illness, ulcers, heart attack, bad back, migraines, and any number of ailments in an attempt to elicit sympathy and to keep their victims in a perpetual spin cycle of trying to figure out what to do.)

In 2004, the lien holder of the promissory note for ten-grand for the failed restaurant decided to foreclose on my house. We had never made one payment on that note because the prince had assured me that he had made an agreement with her that we could just pay her $6,000 when we sold the house, whenever that was. Although I was skeptical about these claims, whenever I pushed him for more details, he would get aggressive and nasty and tell me that he had worked it out; what more did I want? Of course, I stopped challenging him and prayed that he was telling the truth. However, according to the foreclosure documents, I no longer owed her ten-grand but rather $18,000 with the interest, and her attorneys wanted another $12,000 in legal fees. I was looking at homelessness and losing everything I had because of this idiot I was married to.

After meeting with two mortgage brokers about doing another refi and getting turned down, I came home and flopped on the bed, wondering what the hell was going to happen and where would I go if I lost my house. I started thinking about how my life had gone to shit since he came into it and it became unbearable. I started crying and couldn't stop. I hadn't cried like that since I was ten years old and my little dog Dixie Cup got run over by a car. I was inconsolable and so overwhelmed by all the events that I couldn't do anything but sob. He walked into my room and stood over me, yelling at the top of his lungs, "WHAT IS WRONG?" Was he kidding? We were about to lose everything and he wanted to know what was wrong?

I looked at him and said, "We're in this shit because of your deceit and lies. And you've left the entire problem to me to solve. I don't see you asking to borrow money from your family or any of your wealthy friends. You've just left the whole mess to me. I am overwhelmed and can't deal with this stress."

The next thing I knew he was bent over me as I lay on the bed and started screaming at the top of his lungs, "WHAT DO YOU WANT ME TO DO?" He must have yelled that ten times in a row, each time getting louder and angrier. His face contorted in rage and all I could do was cry uncontrollably.

Finally, I screamed back at him, "What do I want you to do? I want you to shut the fuck up and leave me alone! You are absolutely no help."

The next thing I knew he called a friend and asked him to come over and talk to me. I heard him tell the friend on the phone that I was out of control and he didn't know what to do. A half hour later the friend showed up. I went into the living room and sat on the sofa next to him, my face all red and swollen, with snot running down my face. The friend said, "You two must be kind to each other. Love will save everything. . . ." The friend had no idea that we were facing a financial crisis of his doing but he tried very hard to soothe me. After ten minutes of listening to his love lecture, I went back to bed and collapsed.

Thankfully, I had a guardian angel who arranged for me to get an emergency refi to pay off this $31,000 debt, but of course, he wound up yet again on my house deed. The war of attrition began. The house I had owed less than $40,000 on when I met him had climbed to $143,000 with the two re-fis. Things did not get better between us, despite him telling me that he was doing the best he could do. If anything, things escalated. There was fight after fight, threat after threat, with him saying he was leaving but only if he got some money out of me. That just made me dig in my heels because the bastard came into the relationship with nothing, couldn't hold a job, couldn't keep a partnership together, and everything was everyone else's fault, and now I owed $100,000+ more on my house than I had before he waltzed into my life. I was determined not to give him a dime.

By a strange set of circumstances that could only be described as a miracle, I came into a large windfall in December 2004. On more than one occasion he made allusions to how that money would be spent. I suggested that it be used to move out of the country and build a house. After all, we'd been looking in different areas of Colorado, Oregon, Wyoming, Utah, and Montana for years because it became a reality that without him earning any income except for his part-time work which was sporadic, and his Social Security disability which was only $300 a month, we could no longer afford to live in Colorado. My ability to earn a substantial living was dwindling. But more importantly, I had to get the money away from him. I had to save my life. I wasn't getting any younger and working as I had in the past was out of the question. My greatest fear was winding up old, destitute, and homeless – all of which seemed to be looming on the horizon as long as he had anything to say about it. It boiled down to my having a plan that I intended to execute regardless of the consequences.

One night, I spent three hours crunching numbers – doing income projections, factoring in whatever I could get out of my house, even selling my artwork and jewelry. No matter how I worked those numbers, it became patently clear that the only way I would be able to survive – with or without him – was to have a house that was completely paid for. I didn't get enough in Social Security Disability to cover all my expenses if I had to pay rent or a mortgage. The settlement I received was not nearly enough to pay off the mortgage on the Colorado house, but it *was* enough to buy or build a small house in a third world country. And that became my plan. But first, I needed to renew my passport.

"Are you going to change your name on it?" the prince asked as I was filling out the application form.

I had been using my ex-husband's name since 1982, and it had marquee value in the entertainment industry. "It's a big hassle to change your name. There're probably twenty-five different entities I would have to contact to do that. It's tedious and time consuming," I replied, and continued with the form.

"But we're married. You should be using *my* name and not your ex-husband's."

"I could use your last name, just not change it legally."

"But it's a Jew name. It doesn't serve you anymore and if you're going to get a new passport, I think you should change it. In fact, I'm insisting that you get rid of that name. I don't like being married to someone whose last name is Jewish."

PRETTY PINK PALACE, OR PRISON?

January 2005

I made the first trip to Costa Rica with a girlfriend. We had twelve days to move around the country and look at different areas from the quaint mountain towns to the beach communities. On day five, we were staying in the middle of a beautiful valley, surrounded by sugar cane plantations and coffee *fincas*. It was so beautiful and actually very much like the area in Colorado where I lived. I fell in love. It felt like home. Ever since the land deal in Baja California went sideways, I was at a loss of where else to consider. Costa Rica wasn't Mexico, but it was close enough.

The second morning we were there, the developer who owned the B&B we were staying at asked me if I wanted to take a walk to the top of the hill where he had some lots for sale. We hiked to the summit that overlooked a deep valley through which a major river meandered. There were two other houses under construction. But the view! It had me. It could've been Provence, or Tuscany, or Napa Valley. It didn't take a hard-sell to convince me that this was a near-perfect place so I bought a half-acre lot on which to build a house. After I did a handshake deal with the developer, I sent the prince an email that said, "Hi: I just bought a lot here. It's beautiful. Up on a ridge, lovely view of the valley. Looks like Provence, or Napa. I'm going to build a house. If you want to come, great! If you don't want to come, well, that's fine, too, I guess." I was excited because I finally saw a way out.

When I got back, he was less than enthused. Hostile even. After years of talking about leaving and moving someplace cheaper it became apparent that he had no intentions of doing this, and his reluctance to help me build the house only cemented my suspicions that he had designs on that money and was pissed that he wasn't going to get any of it because I had moved it out of the country and out of his reach. There was no way this marriage could hold together much longer, so the house I was building was my only hope of having a place to live when it did end. But somewhere in my heart, I hoped that I was wrong about my suspicions. I didn't want to let go of the dream he had painted for me in the beginning of our relationship. I didn't want the marriage to fail even though it was obvious that's where it was headed if things didn't change. I still wanted to believe in the fairy tale of the perfect marriage, the idyllic life in the countryside, a peaceful existence with very little stress, with a loving and supportive life partner.

All of 2005 and most of 2006 I was back and forth every four or five weeks to check on construction. There were so many things to attend to. When I came home from one of these trips, I would try to engage him in a conversation about the progress of the house, and asked for his input. He had none. Had no interest whatsoever in the design or construction process even though he claimed time and time again that he knew all about building a house.

"Oh, come on," I would plead. "You'll love the lot and the little town. It has everything you said you wanted if you moved out of Colorado. And besides, your Spanish is better than mine. I simply don't know all that construction vocabulary."

"No! I don't want to go there. This was *your* idea; you want to build a house; *you* do it."

"But this is what you said you wanted when we started looking at other areas. This is what we discussed when we bought the land in Mexico. This could be that new beginning that you are always promising me will happen but doesn't. Won't you even come and have a look?"

"Am I speaking Chinese? I said no. You want a house there, well, you build it. I don't want to move to Costa Rica."

"Wow! Well, if you're going to be that way, then I will build it. All by myself."

By October 2006, the house, which was painted a bright pink, was finished and I officially moved in. I was standing in the living room one night, marveling that the house was finished when I realized that it was an almost identical floor plan as the house in Colorado, just a lot bigger. He refused to come down to see what I had accomplished. I went about buying furniture and having draperies made. I was blissfully happy that the hard part was done. The house was beautiful, and it gave me a great sense of satisfaction to know I had accomplished my goals despite all the obstacles he put in my path. Finally, there was a crucial juncture – I had hired someone to pursue legal residency so we wouldn't have to leave the country every ninety days to renew our visas. It was now mandatory that both of us present ourselves to the local authorities and submit to an examination and fingerprints that would be sent to local authorities and Interpol. He wasn't the least bit happy about having to do this, but I insisted and he finally capitulated. He made his displeasure known every single minute of the six days we were there together. At this point, I didn't care. I was proceeding on the path I had created that would allow me to live in a foreign country legally.

In 2007, I came into another large sum of money, which went to finish the details on the house. He was pissed.

"I just want you to know that I don't agree with what you have done. I don't want to leave Colorado. I like it here."

"I like it here, too, but the circumstances we have encountered have made it impossible for us to live here with the money we currently have. You only work part-time, and the same for me. We now have a mortgage payment of over a $1000 a month, and neither of us gets enough in Social Security to afford to live in this house and pay all the other bills. I've shown you the numbers a half dozen times. Moving out of the country is a prudent thing to do because I have no intentions of becoming old, broke, and homeless! For us to continue living here, we would both have to work until we dropped dead. I don't know what your problem is; we could have a nice life there. Without any financial pressure."

None of my arguments mattered to him. He had his own agenda. The threats of divorce were coming on a regular basis.

"Good," I would reply, "but you have to sign my house back to me."

"I don't want your fucking house," he would scream. "It's a stupid stick house anyway. Give me the papers and I will sign them."

I would print out the Quitclaim Deed, give it to him, and he would balk. "I'm not signing anything without consulting a lawyer."

"Go ahead, you do that," I would tell him. "This was *my* house when you met me; all you did was deplete my equity with your crazy schemes. I want my house back!"

"I have rights, you know. I did work on this house. I need to be compensated."

"Are you my husband or a hired worker? Most of the time you lived with me, you rarely contributed to our expenses. The least you could do was some of the repairs. I couldn't afford to pay someone after paying all our bills."

The Quitclaim Deed never got signed. We must have gone through that scenario at least ten different times. The most important thing was keeping the house in Colorado until it could be sold. When Obama got elected there was a mortgage modification program which luckily, we qualified for. I did all the paperwork and if approved, it would drop the mortgage payment by about $350 a month, which of course I was paying because he had no income other than Social Security Disability. It took five months for the loan modification to be approved. During that time, he lived in the house in Colorado and I lived here. It was a peaceful five months, but it started a pattern that would continue for several years.

August 2007 – diary entry

I've been in Colorado the last three months. The house in Costa Rica is rented to a friend of mine while he is building his house in another development a few miles away. I hadn't planned on renting the house but he needed a place to stay and I didn't want to leave the house unattended for four months. It turned out to be a good arrangement for both of us.

Today I went to Denver to do some shopping and when I got into the car and reached beneath the front seat to retrieve the key, I found the ticket that was there. I looked at it and saw the date – it was more than two months old and had been issued because the car didn't bear the current registration sticker on the license plate. I put the ticket in my purse and headed for Denver, but not before I got out of the car and inspected the back plate where I saw the current sticker in the upper right-hand corner. When I got back from town, I asked him about it.

"I found this in the car," I said, waving the ticket in the air.

"What's the big deal?"

"I don't know if it's a big deal. You got stopped and were issued a ticket. It says here that it's a twenty- dollar fine. Did you pay it?"

"No. Why would I pay it? I put the sticker on the car so that automatically cancels out the ticket."

"How do you figure that?"

"That's how it works. Don't worry about it. It's nothing."

If the prince says something is nothing that means it is something he made up or chooses to ignore, fabricating his own version of how it should work in the prince's perfect world. Such as the time he told me (back in 1992) that I didn't need to file my income taxes that year and could wait until next year to do it. Whatever possessed me to believe him is still a mystery. I had never ever in my life not filed my tax return by the deadline. I paid my accountants exorbitant amounts of money to keep me out of debtor's prison. But he spoke so authoritatively that I believed him. Besides, I didn't have the eight grand I owed the IRS so I planned on making a payment arrangement, and he insisted it wouldn't be a problem. It turned out to not be a problem at all – except for the four grand penalty they slapped on the eight grand I owed them. I'd be making payments for a decade now.

The next day, on the pretense of going to the rec center to work out and doing errands, I made a side trip to the traffic division at the courthouse and presented the clerk with the outstanding ticket. She looked at it curiously and retreated to the back room to check if it had been paid. She returned a few minutes later with a sheaf of papers in her hand.

"It appears the ticket was *not* paid and is still outstanding."

"Okay, I can pay that," and fished a twenty dollar bill out of my purse and laid it on the counter. "The sticker is now on the car, so there isn't an issue anymore."

"Great! There's only one small problem."

"What's that?"

"This ticket was issued in May, and it's now August, so it's not twenty dollars anymore."

"How much is it?" I asked, as I watched her flip through the multiple page document she had in her hands.

"It's eighty dollars."

"Goddammit!" I muttered to myself. "What's that you're looking at so intently?"

"This is your husband's driving record."

"May I please see that?"

"Sure. It's public record."

I flipped through eight full pages of driving offenses: Speeding, drunk driving, more speeding, no license, expired license, driving recklessly, illegal parking, running a red light, illegal lane change, and other than vehicular homicide, he had had a ticket for just about every kind of driving violation there was. On page four, there was an entry about the thirty days he spent in the slammer, not just for the driving offense, but for contempt of court and disrupting proceedings. My knees were knocking against the counter. Now I understood perfectly why the insurance company had put that exclusion on my policy. He was basically a danger on the road and uninsurable. I rifled through my wallet and counted out sixty more dollars. When I got back to the car, I just sat there. Fuming. Wondering how many years in prison I would get for justifiable homicide. I took the back road – the scenic route – up the mountain and cranked up the radio, rolled down the windows, and tried to enjoy the beautiful scenery before I went home to have another confrontation.

"I paid your goddamn ticket! It was eighty dollars. Why didn't you just pay it when you got it? Oh, wait. That would be too easy and too responsible."

He said nothing. Just stared at me. I put the sacks of groceries on the kitchen table. I made the decision right then and there that I would never get into another car with him driving.

As was his custom, he stomped off down the hallway and went into his room. I followed him and said, "What is your problem? You got a ticket, didn't pay it, left it for me to find and take care of, and instead of it costing twenty dollars it was eighty dollars. If anyone should be mad, it's me!"

"I just want peace. Why can't we have peace?" He was lying on his bed, staring at the ceiling, and refusing to look at me as I stood in the doorway.

"Peace? If you want peace, you might want to look at your behavior as the reason you don't have that. And besides, peace isn't something you buy at Safeway. It comes from within, and you wouldn't know peace if it slapped you in the head. You thrive on chaos and turmoil and drama. I like peace, too, but I haven't had much of it since you came into my life."

"Then end it. Go ahead."

"I don't want a divorce necessarily. I just want you to stop doing stupid shit!" I turned on my heels and slammed the door after me.

Ten minutes later he came out of his room and came up behind me as I was standing at the sink washing some dishes. He put his arms around my waist and nuzzled my neck. "I'm trying so hard to do things right. But it doesn't seem that I can according to you."

I stood there, frozen. Then he started kissing my neck and turned me around to face him. He pulled me tight to him and stroked the back of my head. "I love you, you know that.

Let's not fight about something so silly. We wouldn't have any problems if you just didn't get so mad. Agree?"

"Okay," I murmured, silently thinking to myself, *it's all my fault for getting upset that he has basically ruined our lives, and I should just shut up about the crazy shit he does.* At that exact moment a wave of paralyzing fear shot through me that I had never experienced before in my life. As he held me and stroked my hair, visions of him breaking my neck went through my mind. I stiffened and disengaged his embrace. I told him I was sorry for getting so mad and resumed washing the dishes. He walked out the door and didn't come back until nine hours later. During the time he was gone one thought rambled through my head: Which one of us was getting out of this marriage alive?

November 2007 – diary entry

After my mother died in 2001, I took some old silver coins she had stashed. Their face value was somewhere around forty dollars, but their numismatic value was much higher. I put them in an old sock, hid them in a box, and stashed it under my bed. One day I went to get something from that box and noticed that the old sock was nearly empty. They'd been there just a few weeks before when I had retrieved something else from that box. The prince was gone - who knows where - so I went into his bedroom and opened the top drawer of his nightstand. There I found five silver dollars. I picked up his passport and two more fell out. Also, among his odds and ends was a pin I had bought in Alaska forty years ago that was encrusted with gold nuggets. I had nearly forgotten I even owned that. Now it made sense that he had probably also stolen my 18k gold watch that had been missing; a watch I had had for more than thirty years and which I had planned to leave to my daughter. My heart started racing so wildly that I had to lie down. Why was he doing this? Why couldn't he just leave my things alone? I had to calm down because if he had walked in the door at that moment, I don't know what I would have done. I found a nearly empty bottle of Xanax and took one, then lay down until I got control of myself. When I heard him come in the front door, I got up and approached him.

"Look what I found in your drawer. My mother's coins. You stole them from me!"

"I didn't steal anything," he snarled. "You gave those to me!"

"Why would I give you my mother's coins? That doesn't even make any sense."

"Why are you always accusing me of stealing?"

"Because my things are always missing and only you and I live in this house, that's why!"

His response was typical. He walked into his bedroom and slammed the door. And that was the end of the conversation. This became the pattern of our relationship. It was on again off again for a decade. With every threat of divorce, I would feel relief that it would soon be over, but he would hoover me back in with his proclamations of undying love, promises about a brighter future, promises that he would always stand by me and that he loved me so much he would take a bullet for me. (I had no idea at the time that hoovering was a typical narcopath tactic to keep the victim from leaving. Most empaths want to believe that the narcopath has seen the light and their promises will come to fruition.)

Saturday, January 26, 2008 – diary entry

I'm back in Costa Rica. Yet again I awoke from very bad and disturbing dreams about his lies, deceit, and anger. In one dream he had put all my orchids in very bright, hot sun and killed them all. When I asked why he did that, he started screaming at me that he liked himself and would do whatever he pleases. There is a pattern in my dreams that he is always killing something, at least this time it was only my orchids and not me. I've had frequent nightmares since I've been down here, and even before, that he intends to kill me. The significance of this theme is that in reality he *is* killing me, emotionally, spiritually, physically, and financially. In the eleven days since I've been here, I've lost at least five pounds just from the GI distress and the inability to eat any solid food. I know the other health symptoms I'm having are synonymous with adrenal burnout from years of living with constant stress and always having to watch what I say and do for fear he unleashes his wrath. It's worse than living with Attila the Hun. At first I felt a sense of relief just from getting away from him, but all the damage he's inflicted on me is still there and surfaces in my dreams. He's even robbing me of my precious sleep. Other than that, I have been very happy here, very much at peace with myself and having great satisfaction with how the house is coming together. It's truly the nicest house on the hill and the best part is that it's all mine, as the house in Colorado once was, only this time this house will always be just mine because I do not trust him to not do something that will cause me to lose it, or at the very least encumber it as he convinced me to do with the other house to subsidize his follies. Why I ever fell for that I'll never know but it will never happen again. I have only myself to blame for enduring year after year of abuse from this guy. I don't understand how he can't see that his rage has destroyed his marriages and any chance at real success. It's starting to make sense what the psychiatrist said about him – that he had deep seated psychiatric problems *before* the accident, including a thought disorder.

One of his favorite stories to tell people is how he got into a fight with someone in a local bar, left the bar, went home and got his gun, came back and waited for the guy to leave the bar and then shot him in the knee. I never really believed the story because it made no sense, and yet he repeated it often to me and to other people. What does someone do after they've been shot in the knee? Go home and put a bandage on it? No! They go to the ER and gunshots are automatically investigated, so obviously the whole story was a lie. But why would anyone tell that story? Yesterday, when I had lunch with a friend, we both agreed that it's his need to feel empowered and important because of his own self-hatred and low self-esteem – why else would he constantly scream at me, "I like myself!" Nobody with self-esteem says that. And the constant anger he has at his mother over her indiscretions going back nearly fifty years. That's a long time to hold a grudge, especially when his other marriage ended because of his screwing around and drug use, so he's nothing but a hypocrite. Soon I'll be free of all of this, but will I ever get my old self back in time to enjoy my life in Costa Rica before I die? I don't know some days. I do truly hate him for how he's treated me, but I let it happen. I should never have let him worm his way back into my house in 1995. I'd thrown him out and then listened to his lies and bullshit about how things will be better and how we would have this fabulous and idyllic life in Italy (talk about future faking!) and now it's thirteen years later and I'm a shadow of my former self, and struggling to regain my sanity and cast off the cognitive dissonance. Despite all the obstacles, I am now living the life I've dreamed about for thirty years.

Sunday January 27 – diary entry
He called yesterday and had that same depressed tone of voice he always has. It's a quiet voice, an attempt to mute his underlying rage. It wound up being a terse conversation. He didn't say he missed me and I didn't say it either because when I hung up I realized I had the same anxiety I have in the States and it's the fear that he will yell or scream at me because the soft, gentle voice is part of the mask. The anxiety dissipated immediately when I realized I was safe and far

away from his rage. And last night, for the first time in a long time, I did not have bad dreams about him.

January 28, 2008 – diary entry

Last night was the worst. I woke myself up screaming after dreaming about him and all the abuse he's heaped on me in seventeen years. My entire body was shaking and I had this pervasive sense of doom, that any second something horrible was going to happen. As these incidents play over and over again in my head, I realize now that the abuse started very early in our relationship. They weren't the isolated incidents I told myself they were. They were a continuing pattern of abuse and control and I was too stupid to believe what I suspected all those years as I listened to him tell me he was sorry and it will never happen again. . . at least not until the next time. And there was always a next time. It's only been since I've had Costa Rica to escape to that I've realized over the past two years just how pervasive and damaging the abuse has been. I have myself to blame for letting it continue as long as I did and had I not been so compromised by the so many extraneous events, I would've gotten out of this sick relationship years ago. But in the early years, I was determined to make it work. I considered it a lifelong commitment and I didn't want to give up on the dream that I had finally found a soul mate and someone I would grow old with. He constantly told me that I was too critical, too hard on him, too strict and at one point I started to believe that maybe it was all me! So, when he borrowed my car at the beginning of a massive snowstorm, telling me he had to go see his daughter at his ex-wife's house, I said nothing. Just handed him the keys, but secretly wondered what could be so important that he had to go out in such awful weather. I kept quiet, and said nothing confrontational when he called three hours later from the neighboring town twenty-five miles away and nowhere near his ex's house, telling me he had locked the keys in the car and would I call a locksmith to come to the Trail-End Bar and unlock the car. After several phone calls, I finally found someone who would go rescue him for $100, which I had to put on my credit card. Even when he straggled in two hours later, I bit my tongue and acted as if everything was just fine. He had trained me well by now. That was just one of dozens of similar incidents that I was not allowed to question, if I knew what was good for me. He had trained me to be complacent and silent.

For the first time, I'm finally feeling grounded enough to put an end to it – as he always told me to do. I've stopped dwelling on all of this during my waking hours but in my sleep it all comes rushing at me like a bad movie and upon waking I feel as though I've experienced the abuse all over again. It's devastating as I don't know how to get these incidents out of my head and my heart. It's a sad reality to realize I've been married to a liar and an abuser for twelve years, plus the five years before that. I'm not willing to give him another year of my life to destroy. My *new* life is in Costa Rica and when we sell the house in Colorado, I'll have a small stash of money plus my Social Security to live on. I should have a very nice life, considering the house here is paid for. I used to feel pity for him, but now I only feel disgust and revulsion at how he's treated me which I suspect was pretty much the same way he treated the ex. I've taken my wedding ring off because it's is the first step in the mental divorce. As easy as that sounds, it's going to be a whole lot harder to heal my psyche.

For years I've kept it secret of how his treats me, more ashamed than anything that I've tolerated it. Besides, who was I going to tell, other than the therapist? My dearest friend Anna made it very clear that she didn't want to hear anymore until I had extricated myself from his grip. It only took a couple of years before he had alienated my friends and isolated me from everyone else. He presented himself as the talented artist, famous chef, all-round good guy willing to help anyone at any time, life of the party, joke teller, *bon vivant*, and of course, the sophisticated, urbane prince! He achieved mythical status. I was relegated to background noise. Of course, he denies that screaming at me is abuse and for years I believed him. Now that I've come clean to two different friends, both of whom suspected something wasn't right in the castle when we were here last January, I feel as though there is light at the proverbial tunnel. They both said the same thing – that it *is* abuse and his denial of it is just another way to manipulate me. It's actually called gaslighting, and he was a master at that. I suddenly feel liberated from carrying the burden of this secret.

Tuesday – diary entry
Wide awake at 5:15 AM – slept well for the first time in two weeks.

Wednesday – diary entry
Another tortured night filled with incomprehensible dreams that I forget immediately upon waking but still feel the effects the next day. Yesterday I met Lynn at the new internet café and then we went to lunch at our favorite restaurant. I had intended to spend an hour or more writing to him but I realized I had nothing to say. *Basta*! My dreams last night were of him breaking things – glasses, decanters, plates, dishes. He has a total lack of respect for things, especially if they belong to me, such as the time he left my $300 briefcase somewhere and never made one attempt to get it back. Who knows why he really left it. I'm sure whatever he told me was a complete lie, and he put on a stellar performance of acting all pissed off that I wanted it back. And whatever happened to my gold watch? A watch I'd had for thirty years that somehow disappeared. And what

about that little watch we bought in Wyoming? He didn't really think I believed the bullshit that it fell out of his pocket at the Cabrini Shrine, did he? And what about my antique stools that had been in the storage shed and then one day they had disappeared. When I asked what happened to them, he mumbled something about how we didn't need them and he gave them to somebody. Never mind that they were 18th century reproductions and worth a lot of money and also had sentimental value. Bottom line is that I'm disgusted for letting this drag on and on knowing he's a pathological liar and a sociopath incapable of a deep human emotion except rage. I am completely horrified that I wasted so many years on this man who I don't believe ever loved me in the first place. I was just another source of supply for his narcissism. Our entire relationship from the very beginning was built on lies, mostly the ones he told me and the ones I had to tell to keep him from destroying my life. All I did was clean up one mess after another, and those were just the ones I knew about. God help me for being so stupid. I am ever so grateful that the universe provided the means for me to start a new life in a country I love. That is my only consolation in all of this chaos.

Scribbled on a piece of paper I found in my wallet

I told him today that one of the reasons I hate having sex with him is that I have to look at that dragon tattoo which reminds me of how I caught him lying to me a week after we got married. He said he would have it removed. Yeah, right.

Undated diary entry

Last night my sleep was littered with nightmares about his lies and in my dream, I told him *not* to use the debit card which he did anyway causing checks to bounce, incurring fees, and when I confronted him, he started screaming at me.

I woke up with my hands shaking and feeling sick to my stomach.

January 30, 2009 – diary entry

After getting back from Costa Rica in September it's has been nothing but hell. Every week for three weeks he kept saying he wanted a divorce. I stopped responding emotionally to these threats and would simply gray rock him or say something along the lines of "Great! Please do that! You keep saying you are leaving, but you're still here. Don't hang around because of me!" Of course, this really wasn't about anything other than cracking my equilibrium and waiting for me to offer him some money to leave, which I steadfastly refused to do.

Then we got hired to fabricate a mosaic mural for the Chicago train station. It was a huge project and required precision and stamina, and more than a little perseverance since we were working in a part of the warehouse that had no heat. For me, it was just about doing the job, but he was as nasty as he could be to me, making me cry at least once a day. Finally, I told him I wouldn't work with him anymore, it was too stressful; I was going home. I straightened up my work station, put the tools away, grabbed my purse and headed for the door. He sneered at me and said, "You're not going to sit on your ass and live off *my* money!" I reminded him that I pay most of the bills for Colorado *and* Costa Rica and walked out the door. I waited until I was nearly home before I burst into tears. Living with this maniac has made me physically ill.

February 15, 2009 – diary entry

The more I think about him stealing those coins from me, the more I realize that I live with a sociopath. I can't wait to get him out of my life. He's done nothing but lie and deceive me, steal my things or break/ruin my things, and try to manipulate and control me. No wonder I've been such a mental wreck for the last twelve years. The PTSD is from living with him. I'm done with his bullshit. It's eighteen miserable years I've put up with his craziness. Why doesn't he just drop dead? Why did I ever marry him? Should I call his sister? She told me twelve years ago that he was crazy and has always had problems and that their father took him to a shrink when he was sixteen after he tried to commit suicide.

February 20, 2009 – diary entry

I'm back in Costa Rica and none too soon. Every time I come here, it more of an escape than anything. All week I've thought about the ways he has tried to control me – one of the most recent ways was telling me *not* to tell *anyone* I had built a house in Costa Rica. He said he wanted to keep his life private; that it was nobody's business, and he didn't want anyone to know. Building a house in another country is exciting and it's an adventure and most people were interested in what I was doing and thought it took a lot of moxie to do it. But over and over again he admonished me to tell nobody. Well, my first act of rebellion was to tell everyone, which of course pissed him off to no end.

This whole week I've gone over every incident in the last seventeen years until it made me feel as though I was coming undone. Part of the pattern of abuse is for him to portray himself as the helpful, outgoing, funny, congenial artist even though most of his jokes are so stupid they're not funny at all. But his favorite trick before any event – whether it's a dinner party or an outing – is to start an argument and then expect me to go to the event and pretend that everything is okay. It's very stressful. At the dinner at Paula and Quinn's house, I made the mistake of sitting next to him. Anytime I started to participate in the conversation, he would poke me hard me on the thigh as a signal for me to be quiet. I usually grab his hand under the table and squeeze it as hard as I can before pushing it away, all the while never missing a beat of what I was saying. After this happened a half dozen times, I always made sure that I sat nowhere near him. Because he puts on this act of being so affable, nobody would think he's emotionally abused me for nearly two decades. I could probably get away with killing him based on this sordid history of abuse.

He just called telling me that same blah blah he's told me for the last five days – that he misses me, loves me, and wants to come home. Just saying he loves me makes my stomach lurch. Now he's making plans to come down here. It will just be the same old abuse all over again. And of course he said he was talking to Lou before he called me, no doubt in an attempt to establish his "good guy" status. If only these people knew what a fraud he is. He might be a good chef and artist, but as a husband and basic human being, he's a piece of shit.

February 21, 2009 – diary entry
A few weeks before I came down here he wanted to know why we weren't having sex. I told him it was just what it is – but what I should've said was "I don't screw liars and thieves!" I knew better than to tell the truth although I had already told him that seeing the dragon tattoo on his arm gave me the creeps. Then he said, "Why did you get married then?" So the only reason I got married was to have sex? What an idiot. (When I queried other abuse victims about why narcissists marry, some of the replies included: Total control, access to your assets, appearing normal or respectable, having a constant supply, having someone to abuse 24/7, etc.)

Every time we did have sex, I suffered through it, hoping for it to be over as quickly as possible because sex was just plain boring and impersonal. He basically reduced it to another bodily function like pooping or peeing. In the early stages of our relationship he would look deep into my eyes and for a brief moment I thought this was to make a spiritual connection and create intimacy. But in truth, he was looking through me, reading my emotions and mirroring them back to me. He wasn't really feeling what I was feeling; he was tricking me, destroying me. And I was falling in love. In the end, it made me feel violated and soul raped. Almost without fail, I would wind up with a urinary tract infection. I had no idea why this occurred on such a regular basis, but it seemed that I was always taking antibiotics, either as a prophylactic, or as a treatment. Never had this problem before. Surely it must be my fault.

March 1, 2009 – diary entry

Another week of being deathly ill and in bed – on antibiotics and two other meds for stress. By Thursday, I knew what the doctor said was true – that this marriage is killing me. "Do you love this man so much that you are willing to let him destroy your health? Surely you know that you are in a dangerously abusive marriage." On Thursday I told the prince I had to divorce him to save my life; that I couldn't handle the abuse or the stress anymore. He said he didn't think he was *that* bad. Haven't heard from him since. I spent eighteen years of my life with a misogynistic sociopath whose only interest in women is to exploit, abuse, and control them. Ugh!

Basically, I've had a complete mental and physical breakdown which started the first day I arrived. Now it's time to put myself together and get on with life. In five days, I have a birthday and I would bet any amount of money that he forgets, just like so many years before. He always claims he can't remember dates but I know that's a lie. I'm going to buy myself something nice as a gift to me.

March 15, 2009 – diary entry

Had a dream last night that a famous preacher wanted me to write an article for him. When I asked him what my compensation would be he said he had two Barry Manilow albums that he would give me that had doubled in value.

Monday – diary entry

He told me he "talked" to his psychiatrist, but the truth was that he racked up another $200 office visit that Medicare won't pay for. This month alone he had $840 in medical bills that are out of pocket – $280 to the dentist, $200 to the shrink, $300 for physical therapy, $60 for the GP. And then there are the dentist bills here in Costa Rica, which will total in the thousands by the time he is done. He's such a hypochondriac. I've never met anyone who had so many ongoing complaints about physical ailments even though he appears healthy as a horse. If I knew then what I know now, I'd have made him have a complete exam, as people do when they are buying a horse! I've thought for years that he goes doctor shopping as a way to spend my money.

March 17, 2009 – diary entry

No fucking sleep. It's been two months of being sick, stressed out, taking meds to control my heart rate and lower cortisol, then antibiotics, and on and on and on – I feel as though I am permanently broken and no matter how hard I try I'll never recover. I really need a therapist to help me put myself back together but I can't afford it. Not even here.

March 23, 2009 – diary entry

Had the worst dream. Was still married to Steve and was getting ready to go to Central America and I asked him where my little dog was and he said, "Oh, I gave him to someone on Craigslist."

"You gave away my sixteen-year-old dog? Why would you do that?"

"I don't know," he shrugged.

"Well, get him back."

"I can't – I don't know where he is."

"Well, you must have some paperwork, how did you send the dog?"

"I put him on a Continental flight and just handed him to the pilot."

Then I started going through drawers of paperwork trying to find the guy's name in the Midwest but found nothing and I was crying hysterically when I woke up and my heart hurt.

Sunday March 29, 2009 – diary entry

Woke up feeling adrift – like I don't belong here or anywhere. He will be here on April 21 and I am having a lot of anxiety about that and while I hope things go well I only have to look at the past to know they won't. I wish he would just go away. I am so happy without him because I have no stress. My life is my own and I can do what I want when I want. The absence of stress has made me realize just how bad it really is. I feel so calm all the time – no trouble sleeping, no Xanax in over two months, and no anxiety at all. It just confirms that all my health problems are caused by external forces.

June 7, 2009 – diary entry

He was only here five weeks and this is the first day I haven't felt as though I was going to blow apart. The short time he was here was just like all the other times, except that we didn't have any nasty fights until the end when I discovered that he'd smoked all the pot I had hidden. He told me he threw it in the trash because it was moldy and if I didn't believe him to look in the trash. I did look and of course there wasn't any pot. We had a couple of nice outings to the hot springs, and he did sand and varnish the pillars and hung the house sign. Some days I thought he was really trying but when I discovered the pot was gone, I knew nothing had or would change. A four-year-old learns you don't lie, steal other peoples' things or break them, but he doesn't seem to "get" any of that.

June 27, 2009 – diary entry

I love living in Costa Rica in a house I built, overlooking a huge valley of sugar cane plantations. I'm sitting here pinching myself, wondering how I got to be so lucky to have all of this. Could my life here by anymore perfect? But life is very strenuous if you're going to do basic maintenance – there's the inside, outside, the orchard, the garden, the compost pile, the terrace – that's a full day's work and then some. But I don't mind when I'm here alone and not being mentally tortured by the sociopath I'm married to. This house is my insurance policy that I will always have a place to live. After going through the stress and turmoil of a foreclosure, I never, ever want to feel that sense of insecurity again. I'm just happy that I had the foresight and tenacity to do this over his objections, temper tantrums, and abuse. When it became patently obvious that his plan was to destroy any financial security I had, the only choice I was left with was to forge ahead on my own and make sure that my future was secure. Without that, I risked losing everything and being homeless.

November 13, 2009 – diary entry

He's been back a month. I thought he would stay in Colorado but he insisted that he wanted to come "home." All he does all day is sit on the computer, doing what I have no idea.

November 16, 2009 – diary entry

That lying bastard. Three days ago, I was doing computer stuff in the living room and he was sitting at the dining room table with his laptop. He kept asking me how to spell words. I figured he must be writing to someone he wanted to impress because he seemed really engrossed in what he was doing and truth be told, he is the worst speller, even in his first language. And if he's writing English it's almost indecipherable. He really *can't* spell a three-letter word! Twice he told me in an agitated tone, "Don't read my email!" Until today I had never snooped in his emails, but I started thinking what was it he didn't want me to see? When he went to bed, I logged onto his AOL account. At first, I felt guilty about doing this, until I found the emails he didn't want me to see. He had written several emails to Linda Smith telling her he could feel her skin, how she is his only soul mate, and would she please meet him in Sardinia so they could continue their old romance, how he misses her kisses, etc. Whew! Guess he's trying to line up his next supply. Could I be so lucky? Reading all of that made me sick to my stomach. I have no doubt now that he's cheated on me. She wrote back and said she was flattered, but that she was happily married, and their affair had been a long time ago, when she was very young. I decided to say nothing about reading his emails, but after finding several other disturbing pieces of correspondence, I set up a file and started dropping those messages into it. My hands shook every time I looked at another sent email. He was sending the nastiest messages to people, sometimes outright blackmailing or extorting them. I needed to know what else he had been up to considering that some of these threatening emails could be considered criminal. Since I set up his Facebook account, I have that password, too, and the things I have found there are truly frightening. He insults people, threatens them, sends them private messages that are so abusive that many people banned him or reported him. He is also approaching women and telling them how beautiful they are, how he wants to meet them, and when they ask him personal questions such as does he have a wife or children, he says he has an adult daughter. I don't exist.

December 24, 2009

In a fit of desperation, I contacted Dr. Haylock, the prince's psychiatrist, to tell him that his behavior has been increasingly argumentative, confrontational, insulting, irrational, and just plain obnoxious. I told him he took the coins that belonged to my mother, how I found some of them in his drawers and passport, how he claimed not to remember taking them and how he didn't steal them as I claimed, but rather argued that stealing is when you take something, sell it, and then put the money in your pocket. As soon as I finished telling Dr. Haylock *that,* he said, "He needs to be on an antipsychotic. His thinking is disordered. He is probably depressed and suffers from a high level of anxiety. The antipsychotic should help with these thought patterns." However, he refuses to take any kind of medication. He claims that his status as an Italian citizen affords him certain rights that supersede anything I or his doctors may say regarding his behavior or treatment thereof. Just what the hell is that supposed to mean? Surely, it's more bullshit that he's invented.

Last week he ranted for an hour about faggots and queers, how they were sick, how he doesn't want their behavior shoved in his face. I explained to him that those terms were politically incorrect. His response was, "Those words are in the dictionary and therefore I have the right to use them, just as I have the right to use the word nigger because I was born in West Africa." The frustration of trying to reason with him when he is in that condition is pointless. More importantly, why is he so homophobic? Once I realized that he felt that way, I started to wonder if there was something about him I did not know – such as maybe he was secretly gay. The very next day we were having a party at Jeff's house, who happens to be gay. I feared that he would say something insulting if he had anything to drink, so my edict was that there would be no more drinking, but he demanded that I give him the wine I stashed. I stood firm and said no.

"Fuck off! Wine is a treat for me and since I'm Italian, it's my right to have it!"

By 2010, we were separated four or more months at a time while he was in Colorado supposedly doing work on the house readying it to rent until the market picked up and we could sell it. He also needed to spend a certain amount of time there to meet the Green Card requirements. Larry was the first tenant, but that didn't last long because after a couple of months, the prince threw him out and it cost me hundreds of dollars to have him go away. Then it was rented to another loser the prince knew who got busted for drunk driving and went to jail but not before he had made arrangements to sublet my house to friends of his. He was given the boot. Then came Josie – who was a good tenant, but couldn't afford to pay more than $575 a month which meant the rest of the expenses on the house were paid for by me, since her payment only covered the mortgage. This house was becoming a terrible burden. But the market was still soft and prices were stagnant. It could be two to five years before we could sell it.

I was living full time in Costa Rica, working on various magazine and other writing projects. Then I got a job with a local eco-lodge doing their online marketing. It didn't pay much but it covered a lot of expenses on the house in Colorado. I was given two weekends a month at the lodge as part of my compensation package, and that became my safe haven when he became impossible to deal with. It's what made my life tolerable during this period. Doing social media marketing was a great way to channel my energy while I figured out the rest of my life. It kept me engaged with interesting people and I needed this distraction from my chaotic and insane life.

January 13, 2011 – diary entry

Three times this week he went completely off the rails – belligerent, abusive, irrational. In the past, I have made every excuse there was for his behavior, but I have arrived at the point where I no longer get upset when he goes crazy. I just walk away or stare at him in disbelief. However, it does make me extremely cautious about how I am going to proceed to get him out of my life. This episode was so bad that I wrote to his sister to tell her she has to either talk some sense into him or come and get him. I am more afraid of him now than ever, because crazy people are unpredictable. Someone asked me what in particular was I afraid of and I couldn't answer. It's just this fear that being around him is dangerous; that he is unpredictable, capable of violence, and has no conscience. Isn't that enough?

April 29, 2011 – diary entry

Again and again and again – every time he drinks he turns into an irrational, confrontational asshole. Today's fight was over the hundred dollars Jeff gave me to buy bedding plants for the B&B. "I want that hundred he gave you in my pocket." I explained to him that the money was to buy things, not to put in his pocket. Boy, was he pissed at me.

Then he came up with another scheme: "Why don't we sell the bottom half of the lot to Mike for $25,000?"

"I'll tell you why – because I'm not a fucking idiot!" I had to laugh because it was just another way to squander my assets. "I've already got taken by you for over $100,000 because of your crooked friend and your disastrous business dealings. There is no way I am going to sell half of my property to one of your friends so you can latch on to the proceeds."

One of the smartest things I did, when I was able to think clearly, was have him sign a power of attorney after his auto accident. He had made such a case about being disabled and incapable of doing anything requiring critical thinking that I told the lawyer that it was imperative I have a POA. He is going back to Colorado and I simply don't trust him not to do something that imperils us financially by putting the house, which is in both of our names, at risk. With the POA I can legally transfer it into my name only. I don't see any other way of protecting myself from his careless and reckless behavior.

May 13, 2011 – diary entry
I went to the lawyer today to get a Quitclam Deed notarized so I can transfer the house in Colorado into just my name. I have nightmares and am scared to death of what he will do to jeopardize that property based on what I have seen in his emails and Facebook messages. He clearly has another life other than the one he has with me. As his emails and Facebook messages have revealed, he is a spiteful, vindictive person. Will he burn down the house, will he blow it up, will he steal some of my valuable things that are in the storage shed? One of my big fears is that he will rack up a bunch of debt and there will be liens against the property. I have good reason to be concerned; after all, in the twenty years we've been together, the IRS already attached my bank account once. He is a very dangerous person and I am afraid of him and have had dreams of him killing me. I truly believe that he fits the sociopath profile. He doesn't seem to have any remorse about his actions, or even guilt. He is just out for

himself and will do anything to get what he wants. The next two weeks are going to be very difficult, but I have to make sure that the Deed gets filed and registered before he goes back to Colorado. It would not surprise me if he tried to throw the tenant out so he can move back in, and the only way I can make sure that doesn't happen is to take him off the Deed so he has no right to do so.

Nobody is designed to live with this constant stress. I can see the changes in my skin and my facial structure from cortisol overload. The constant racing heart and pounding head, is, as the doctor told me, a formula for either a heart attack or a stroke. So, I have to make it through the next two weeks before I can get him out of here. And once he is gone, I never want to see him again, and there is no way he will ever set foot in this house in Costa Rica. If I have to sell the house in Colorado, well, so be it, but it will be when I decide not when he wants me to, and if he thinks he is going to get anything else out of me, he's got another thing coming. As far as I am concerned, he owes *me* money. I know he only married me for what he thought he could get out of me and so far, he has managed to do pretty well. Except for maybe one year, I have always contributed more to our lifestyle than he has, and there have been months and months at a stretch where he earned not a dollar. I cannot wait to get this monster out of my life and never have to deal with this lying, stealing, or bullshitting ever again.

May 14 – diary entry
We had a discussion this morning about stealing. I asked him again what he did with my gold watch and he told me he doesn't remember and I told him I consider that he stole it and either sold it for cash or traded it for drugs. He insisted that he did *not* steal it because stealing is when you take something and then sell it, and since he didn't sell it, he

therefore did not steal it. He actually didn't deny taking it in that word salad about the definition of stealing. Something about the way he said that set off alarm bells. When he to went to the airport to pick up his friend Mike, I went into his bedroom and opened up the leather-covered notebook he has and out fell my 24K gold chain with the jade Buddha pendant. That chain had been stashed in the false bottom drawer in a separate pouch with other items, which meant he rifled through everything to find it. With him leaving for Colorado next week, he was most likely going to take it with him and sell it. Had he done that, I never would've known what happened to it, and he would've lied about taking it. What kind of monster am I living with? Every couple of nights before I go to bed, I lock my bedroom door, take out all my jewelry from the hiding place and count everything – the coins, the rings, the bracelets, the gold earrings. I knew when he asked me how to access the false bottom drawer that I had reason to worry. What if I hadn't had a gut instinct to check his things? He would've gotten away with chain made of pure Chinese gold and would've denied that *he* took it. I left a piece of paper on his bed with the definition of stealing. When he returned several hours later, I heard him crumple the piece of paper and throw it in the trash. He didn't make any comment. So far, I have managed not to play my hand, and have said nothing about finding my chain. I have now taken everything of value out of the house and put it where he will never know where it is. I cannot trust my own husband to *not* steal from me. Now I have all the more reason to worry about what is in the storage shed in Colorado. He knows I have my silver service and since he has stolen silverware from houses he worked in, there is no reason for him *not* to steal from me. I'm just wondering what he's going to do when he discovers that the chain is gone.

Next day – diary entry

He woke up and started stomping around the house the way he does when he is trying to terrorize me. He was exuding rage. Said he wanted to go back to Colorado and that's what he's doing in a few days. After slamming doors, muttering under his breath, and stomping through the house, I did the stupid thing of asking what he was so mad about. He started ranting that there is no way he can live on $469 a month from Social Security. I told him he could get a job. I suggested he apply for welfare. He said "I don't think I can get welfare if I own a house." Well, won't he be surprised when he finds out his name is no longer on the house, and if I catch him trespassing, I will have the tenant call the police. I feel sick inside. But I know confronting him will only turn into an ugly insult-slinging match and I am not up for it. I need to just stay calm, wait for this Deed to be registered, and get this jackass out of my life. I wonder what else he has stolen from me over the years. I remember several years ago when I saw him shoplifting from Home Depot, I asked him why he did those things. "There is a saying in the Bible: God helps those who help themselves. I was helping myself." What kind of person justifies stealing by misquoting the Bible? Who thinks like this? Only a sociopath.

This morning there was an article on *HuffPost* about how to identify a psychopath, and lo and behold, he passed the test with flying colors. I bookmarked it. If I can tell he is completely crazy, I wonder how crazy he *really* is. I have eighteen days to survive this nightmare. If I find out that the Quitclaim Deed has been registered sooner than my cutoff date, I will book him an earlier flight. I will also have to take him off the checking account and cancel his debit card. I just don't trust him. I will be the focus of his wrath and he will justify whatever he does to me or my things by saying I abused him. It's like having a monster living in your house. I am afraid to make waves right now. I just have to stay calm, not be argumentative or accusative, and get him out of here as quickly and as easily as I can. My stomach is in knots. How could he do these things? Oh, yeah, I forgot, sociopaths have no conscience, no empathy, and no remorse.

I checked flight prices and they had gone up a hundred dollars in twenty-four hours, so now the fare is $250 and it won't get cheaper, so I booked it for June 3 on Continental. I just hope I can keep it together until then. Right now, I am on autopilot, just doing what has to be done, but completely numb inside and feeling incredibly anxious and depressed about all of this. Not about him leaving, but about the number of years I have spent and wasted believing him, then catching him lying again, and stealing again, and not being able to end it because I was more afraid of what he would do than of staying put. The main thing I didn't want to do was to give him a goddamn nickel after all he's stolen from me and swindled me out of. I will be checking off the days in my mind and will feel nothing but relief that he will be out of my life. I just pray that nothing happens between now and then.

Later same day – diary entry

After he was being particularly contentious and argumentative, I told him I found my gold chain. His response was, "I knew you would. I did it to get attention."

I had to ask the obvious question: "How is stealing a valuable item of jewelry going to get you attention? Isn't that kind of like burning down your mother's house because she isn't paying attention to you?"

The more he tried to explain why he takes my things, the crazier he sounded. It was a total word salad, and none of it made any sense at all. I asked him if he had any kind of conscience and didn't it bother him when he takes my things, didn't it make him anxious knowing all hell is going to break loose when I find out? But halfway into my discussion, I realized that talking to him is useless. He said he wanted to work on things. I told him there wasn't anything to "work" on because *he* is the problem.

"I'm trying to learn from my mistakes."

"Pffft," I scoffed. "Every other time you told me that, I believed you. But need I remind you that you keep making the same mistakes over and over and in twenty years, you haven't progressed very far on the learning curve. I cannot believe that anything will change in the future."

Sunday May 15 – diary entry

This morning, I told him that I booked his flight. "A simple way to do this would be if I came up in July or August and bring you the rest of your stuff."

"Oh, so you want me out of here, is that it?"

"Hey, wait a minute. Stop the goddamn manipulation. This is what *you* said *you* wanted – to go back to Colorado and get a divorce. Are you telling me that isn't what you want now?"

"I'm just mad at the state of our marriage."

"Why do you think things are the way they are and do you feel you had any role in the breakdown?"

"You're always so hard and so strict."

"If I weren't, we would've been homeless a long time ago, with no money and no place to live. You have demonstrated over and over that you are irresponsible and couldn't care less what happens to us – whether we wind up homeless, losing everything, and living where? Under a bridge? And don't give me that shit that you would be happy living in your car because that is *not* an option for me. So yeah, your unfettered access to what is left of my assets has been curtailed and I will continue taking control of our finances whether you like it or not!"

He stormed down the hallway to his bedroom and slammed the door.

Tuesday, May 17 – diary entry

I read his emails. He told his daughter he may have to go to the hospital; that his memory is very bad and he is not feeling well. He also asked her for some survival money until he goes to her wedding in July and that he would arrange things with the ex. Maybe he can move back into her garage. This morning when I asked him how I could ever possibly trust him again after the lies he has told me and the things he has taken from me, he said, ''You have been going on about this for three days! Give it up!''

"No, I'm not giving it up. What you took from me was a necklace worth a minimum of three grand, not a trinket, and what if I hadn't found it, what would you have done with it?"

"I didn't hide the necklace. It was right there," and he pointed to his notebook. I reminded him that he had stashed it in the inside pocket where it wasn't visible so he was *not* to tell me that it was sitting "right there." Then he went on to tell me that for all those months that he was in Colorado he never took anything of mine to sell. He is now making me out to be the bad person because I am upset at catching him in another one of his deceits. At this point I am completely numb. I can't even cry anymore. I feel as though someone reached into my chest and ripped my heart out. I asked him what would change in our marriage if he came back from Colorado. He said he had learned his lesson. I asked him *again* what that was, since he had told me that repeatedly over the years. He couldn't tell me what the lesson was, just that he had learned it, and when I asked him how I was supposed to believe that after all the other lies, he said, "It's up to you."

At this point, if I were to take him back then I would be the crazy one, because nobody should have to live with this type of emotional terrorism. I am supposed to just move on from this incident, act like it didn't happen, and we should continue this totally sterile marriage until one of us dies . . . I guess. So, until he leaves, I just have to stay calm, not provoke him, and keep my bedroom door locked, which is what I did when I left for town today. Now how crazy is that? That to protect myself and my things–not from burglars but from my husband – I have to lock my bedroom door when I leave the house. Is it any wonder that I feel as though I am spinning through space?

July 2011 – diary entry
He wants to come back. He called me and in that calm, quiet voice that I know is a prelude to something awful, he proceeded to tell me that he misses me more than he ever has, that he wants to come "home" (even though he has always said he hated Costa Rica), and that he will try as best he can to make up for all the stress he has caused me. Ugh

Original Message----- From: glxxxxxx sent July 9, 2011 1:23 p.m.

Subject: is this you?

This is why I am afraid to have you come back:

"Profile of the Sociopath. They never recognize the rights of others and see their self-serving behaviors as permissible. They appear to be charming, yet are covertly hostile and domineering, seeing their victim as merely an instrument to be used. They may dominate and humiliate their victims. Feels entitled to certain things as "their right." Has no problem lying coolly and easily and it is almost impossible for them to be truthful on a consistent basis. Can create, and get caught up in, a complex belief about their own powers and abilities. Extremely convincing and even able to pass lie detector tests. A deep seated rage, which is split off and repressed, is at their core. Does not see others around them as people, but only as targets and opportunities. Instead of friends, they have victims and accomplices who end up as victims. The end always justifies the means and they let nothing stand in their way. When they show what seems to be warmth, joy, love and compassion it is more feigned than experienced and serves an ulterior motive. Outraged by insignificant matters, yet remaining unmoved and cold by what would upset a normal person. Since they are not genuine, neither are their promises. Verbal outbursts and physical punishments are normal. Promiscuity and gambling are common. Unable to empathize with the pain of their victims, having only contempt for others' feelings of distress and readily taking advantage of them. Rage and abuse, alternating with small expressions of love and approval produce an addictive cycle for abuser and abused, as well as creating hopelessness in the victim. Believe they are all-powerful, all-knowing, entitled to every wish, no sense of personal boundaries, no concern for their impact on others. Usually has a history of behavioral and academic difficulties, yet "gets by" by conning others. Problems in making and keeping friends; aberrant behaviors such as cruelty to people or animals, stealing, etc. Not concerned about wrecking others' lives and dreams. Oblivious or indifferent to the devastation they cause. Does not accept blame themselves, but blames others, even for acts they obviously committed. Tends to move around a lot or makes all-encompassing promises for the future, poor work ethic but exploits others effectively. Changes their image as needed to avoid prosecution. Changes life story readily. Does not perceive that anything is wrong with them. Goal of enslavement of their victim(s). Exercises despotic control over every aspect of the victim's life. Has an emotional need to justify their crimes and therefore needs their victim's affirmation (respect, gratitude and love). Ultimate goal is the creation of a willing victim. Incapable of real human attachment to another. Unable to feel remorse or guilt. Extreme narcissism and grandiosity. May state readily that their goal is to rule the world (The above traits are based on the psychopathy checklists of H. Cleckley and R. Hare.)

His response: Sent: Thu, Jul 14, 2011 11:14 am Subject: Re: is this you

well you have tu much immagination after all you are e wrighter you make sstory up tu sadisfai your twisted mind lets not weist time on buscit you are not special you wrote a book end I had tu finance it   lets get tu the practical side of the reality wat du you propose in colorado I have wrights the oone hu is not ligal is you did you diclare the house of costa rica you must olso pai my labor end money I have put in the house so tell me wat du you propose I dont want tu get en attorney if I du we bot luse   I dont care if you slept or will slip w the greec   tu me you are like judas you   brock your word I never stole anithing from you ita all in your head I find all this patetc may the great spirit bless you .

My response:

You were more than adequately compensated for whatever work you did on either house – it was the least you could contribute when you had no income. You stole the coins that belonged to my mother. I found them hidden in your stuff. You also stole that 24k gold chain, which I also found stashed in your notebook, not in plain site as you claim. You have stolen other things from me as well such as my Geneva gold watch.   When we sell the house in Colorado at the end of the loan modification in 2014, you will get some small percentage of whatever money there is, and there won't be much.   The first $20,000 from the sale belongs to me.   And when we calculate what you will owe me for your debt on the restaurant in Denver, you could wind up owing ME money.   Your threats and your accusations that I may have slept with Jeff is proof positive that you have some serious problems.   What about him being gay don't you understand?   These accusations are part of the reign of terror you have perpetrated on me for twenty years. No, you do not want to hire a lawyer. If you do, I will claim mental and emotional abuse and fraud for all the lies you told me. The abuse is well documented going back to 1996. You do not want those things to come out in court or for your daughter to find out just what kind of person you really are, although she probably already knows. I am going out of town and will not have access to Magic Jack until the beginning of the week. We will talk then.

June 2012 – diary entry

For the last seven years, I have been managing the house next door to me after the owner returned to the US. It was my responsibility to keep the house rented and to pay all the bills and do whatever work needed to be done. We've had a succession of tenants, some good, some not so good, and we finally got a retired couple who moved in last December. They were really nice and we became friends, having dinners together and going on outings. Everything was just fine until they went back to the States on a vacation earlier this month. One day, the alarm went off. I couldn't figure why that happened – maybe a bird had tripped the motion sensor was my first thought. I went into my house and got the alarm fob that was on the set of keys. I hit the button repeatedly to turn off the alarm but it wouldn't work. The only way to turn it off was to go inside the house and reset the alarm. There were a couple of problems with that and the main one was that the gate to the staircase was too high for me to climb over with the sprained ankle I had. When the alarm went off, I had been standing in the street talking to another neighbor who was also a friend of the tenants. I asked her to help me with the alarm. We went to the front of the house and she took the keys and went inside and reset the alarm. It took less than sixty seconds. I immediately went back to my house and sent the tenants an email and explained what happened and explained why the other neighbor had gone inside to reset the alarm on the keypad. They wrote back that they were happy I took care of it. Three days later they returned. Mrs. X called me to tell me they were back. Then she said she was really upset because someone had gone into their house and rummaged through their drawers and had left the drawer with a false-bottom open by a quarter of an inch. I told her there was no way that the person who reset their alarm would've done that because she was in full view of me the entire time she was in the house. Mrs. X started yelling at me, saying I had done it, and that they never wanted me to set foot on the property ever again while they were living there. I called the owner in California and told him what had happened. Mrs. X also called him and stated that I had burgled their house, rifled through drawers, and that they couldn't trust me and wanted to move. They had done some minor cosmetic things to the grounds and now they were demanding $15,000 in compensation for the improvements so they could move and find another place to live. I was so upset. Nobody had ever accused me of doing such a thing, nor would I because it's not something that would enter my mind. The whole situation was so awful. The tenants went around to other neighbors and told them that I had violated their space, etc. At some point, the prince went over to their house and read them the riot act. Who knows what he told them, but the next thing I knew they were planning on leaving as soon as they could. The owner of the house and I decided that maybe they had made up this story as a way to get some money out of him. We really didn't know. It all seemed very strange to us and we had no way of investigating what had happened and only had their side of the story. The owner, with whom I had been friends for seven or eight years, believed me when I told him I never set foot inside their house. We agreed that there was nothing to do but just let them stay until they found another place to live and continue to collect the rent. It was very upsetting, and it was just one more thing piled on the ever-growing heap of stressors.

July 2012 – diary entry

I finally broke down and bought a car. An old Geo Tracker, good on gas mileage, and with 4-wheel drive. Taking the bus to the farm and back twice a month was starting to wear on me. It's only thirty-two miles to the farm and the trip that takes one hour and ten minutes in a car but takes two and a half hours on the bus. Plus, walking a half mile to the bus stop to go to town was starting to take its toll on my bad knee. I swore I wasn't getting a car ever in this country – driving is incredibly stressful because they all drive like they're drunk – but it finally became a necessity.

When we went to the lawyer's office with the seller to transfer title, Mario explained that there was no such thing as joint ownership here so the car was placed in a "fideicomiso" which is like a trust, with the prince named as the beneficiary but with me holding title. It was my car, and I did not hesitate to let him know that he was never going to drive if I was in the car. I had had enough of his erratic driving - tailgating, blinking the lights, honking the horn, flipping off other drivers, pulling alongside of them and screaming in Italian, and making hand gestures. I warned him numerous times that one day someone is going to pull out a gun and shoot him. It's not like it hasn't happened, and I sure as hell didn't want it happening with me in the car. If we go anyplace together, I drive and there's no discussion.

August 18, 2012 – diary entry

Oh my God, he's having yet another episode but this time he's not sucking me into his spiral of bullshit. He's barely been back from the US a month and already he wants to go back to Colorado. Why now? Because I asked him to please not use my mother's signed Waterford crystal candle holders to light his joints. Never mind that they cost $300 and have sentimental value, or that he is constantly breaking my things. Next thing I knew he was ranting and raving how he can't take it anymore. He wants a divorce, wants to go back to Colorado, wants me to give him some money. It's always the same old routine; next week, he will be all calm and happy and glad we are living here and not in the US. Let's face it, he doesn't have many options – his sister won't help him, his nephews don't want him around, and I am sure as hell not going to allow him to manipulate me again into spending my savings on one of his crazy episodes. Four different times he conned me into sending him back to Colorado only to have him call me several weeks later to hoover me in with is declarations of love and his willingness to change his bad behavior. HA! I'm not doing it again unless he signs the house over to me.

When he came back, he was all smug and arrogant and said to me, "A letter from the County came while I was in Colorado. What you did – trying to screw me out of my portion of your house – was illegal. I have the letter and you could be in big trouble."

I said nothing, but waited until he had left the house and then went through all of his papers and found the actual letter from the county. There was nothing threatening about it, they were only informing me that the rules had changed and now the POA had to be on file before there could be any transactions with the property. So, he was trying to intimidate and scare me. I took the letter and stashed it away. The bitch of it is that the house didn't get transferred and is still in both our names.

This time I did not have a meltdown because I finally saw this as one more episode like every other episode and this is just what narcissists and sociopaths do – their behavior is designed to control and intimidate. (I was doing gray rock before I knew that was an actual strategy). What a fool I was to let him convince me that he was willing to work on the things and that he wanted yet another chance to prove we could have a good marriage. I don't know what I was thinking when I said "okay."

BETWEEN THE SILENCE AND THE MADNESS

September 2012 – diary entry

An episode can last for minutes or days, and a window of normalcy can last for days or months. The more docile I am, the longer the normalcy lasts. The more I push or try to discuss issues I don't agree with, the more likely it will trigger an episode. Yes, it's walking on eggshells, and I am grateful for the windows of sanity until the next episode comes out of the blue. I always refer to these periods as "between the silence and the madness."

His drinking, no matter how little it was, makes him intolerable. He gets even more argumentative, irrational, accusatory, and vicious than he was when sober. I told him I would no longer put up with him drinking. His response is always, "Go fuck yourself, you bitch."

I would respond with, "You are *not* going to talk to me like that in *my* house."

He would look at me murderously, and say, "The lawyer says I own half this house, and half the house in Colorado, so go fuck yourself."

The war had begun.

The other issue that we fought about constantly was his marijuana use. He smoked pot from the time his eyes opened in the morning until he passed out at night. I told him there was no way we could afford his habit and that he had to cut down, but he never did, and he always seemed to have something to smoke. If we did buy a small bag, I would take a portion of it and hide it for my own use. I would put it in places in my bedroom that I didn't think he would ever find, but sure enough when I would go to get some of it, it would be totally gone, or he would leave me just a few crumbs. When I confronted him and told him I didn't like that he was snooping in my things, he denied it, and said I was imagining things. (More gaslighting!) Over the years, I had discovered that rummaging through my personal belongings was a pasttime for him. I knew I had crossed some imaginary line of unacceptability when I started putting tiny pieces of wadded up paper on the inside of my drawers so that if they were opened that little speck would become dislodged. Upon my return from every trip to the farm, I would check those drawers and sure enough, they had been opened in my absence. It finally got to the point where I had to lock my bedroom door when I left the house, but even that didn't deter him. When I left for the farm one weekend, he informed me when I returned home that he had had to break into my room to retrieve the dog I had locked inside. I knew this was a lie because I made sure the dog was not in there when I closed the door. That was just his way of letting me know that nothing could stop him from getting in there and rummaging and/or stealing my things. It was a mind fuck game of major proportions that I didn't even realize had a name or that it was classic behavior from someone suffering from narcissistic personality disorder, or anti-social personality disorder. I didn't even know this was considered abuse, since our standard definition of domestic violence was being hit, punched, or slapped. He never laid a hand one me. I thought I was just being a strong and determined woman, living with a man who had had a traumatic childhood, a bad relationship with his mother, and who now suffered from a brain injury. I was clearly committed to the concept of sticking it out for better or worse, till death do us part. Only after I realized that he fit the classic personality profile of a narcissist/sociopath did I start doing research and discovered that there was a whole lexicon of terms that applied to such behavior:

Emotional Abuse - referred to as psychological violence or mental abuse; involves subjecting someone to behavior which may result in psychological distress or trauma such as chronic depression, stress, anxiety and post-traumatic stress disorder.

False Flattery - Narcissists thrive on adoration and they assume everyone else does, too. They will tell you that you are special, no one can understand them like you do and put you on a pedestal.

Future Faking - the promise of an idyllic future together in order to get what they want from you at this moment.

Enabler - someone who by their action or inaction encourage or enable a pattern of behavior to continue or remove consequences of bad behaviour.

Flying Monkeys - people who have been convinced by the narcissist that he or she is the real victim. They may threaten, torment, discredit or add fuel to a smear campaign by spreading lies and gossip.

Gaslighting - a manipulative tactic where an individual is subjected to conditioning behavior so that they doubt their own sanity. The target starts to believe that their perception of reality is false. The narcissist may simply deny saying something didn't happen, tell you that you heard wrong or lie about an event or situation. A victim starts to think they are confused and going crazy.

Gray Rock - a term used to describe your behavior when trying to cut contact with a narcissist. The aim is to be utterly boring so that the narcissist no longer sees you as good supply and subsequently disappears.

Hoovering - derived from the Hoover vacuum cleaner which describes how a narcissist attempts to suck their victims back into a relationship. They will use every trick in the book to get you back under their power and control. Hoovering often takes place after you have left them or after a period of the silent treatment. They often promise to change their behavior or say that they have already changed dramatically.

Invalidation - a manipulative tactic used to get a target to believe that their thoughts, opinions and beliefs are wrong, unimportant or don't matter.

Love Bombing - a term used to describe the typical initial stages of a relationship with a narcissistic where the narcissist goes all out to impress their target with flattery, holidays, promises of a future together having the target believe that they have met their perfect partner, their soul mate.

Mirroring - what they see in you from your mannerisms to your fashion sense, your behavior, your likes and dislikes. They basically become just like you. They will have the same dreams and hopes as you in an attempt to convince you that they share your reality.

Narcissistic Supply - consists of attention, admiration, respect, adulation, and even fear.

No Contact - put in place by a victim in order to give themselves time to recover. It is not the same as the narcissist's silent treatment which is a punishment and to

exert power and control. No contact is self-imposed and there will be no contact in any form with the toxic person,
Projection - projecting their own character flaws or bad behavior onto others. They are not accountable for any wrong doing and will blame others for the very things that they do themselves.
Scapegoat – someone blamed for just about everything that goes wrong.
Trauma Bonding – derived from a real-life hostage situation where a hostage becomes emotionally attached to their kidnappers – also known as The Stockholm Syndrome. Trauma bonding creates a dependency where the victim is unable to leave an unhealthy or dangerous relationship.

Undated Diary Entry
After more than a decade of abuse, I am shattered. There are days when I can't function at all. I am just going through the motions of life, trying to wait it out until he just picks up and leaves. Sometimes he actually does, but just when I heave a sigh of relief, he petitions me to return with the usual promises of better behavior and no more fights. The only thing that saved me from either killing him or myself was the fact that he had to be in the US a certain number of months a year to maintain his Green Card. I looked forward to these respites and during the time he was gone I saw a glimpse of what life could be without him and his constant chaos. He seemed to thrive on bedlam, and was a drama queen like none I had ever encountered. Eventually, I fell into a pattern of simply avoiding him. We stopped having sex altogether, and I made sure that our conversations were limited to only issues that pertained to our daily life. I became docile and silent. We pretty much started leading separate lives: I had my little job at the eco-lodge, and he had a life I knew nothing about, but would find out much later in the game. My life with him was nothing but turmoil. I knew I had to

end it but I couldn't figure out how to do that without him hosing me financially, which seemed to be his only goal. Most of the time I was in too much distress to even write about what was happening, but when I read these diaries, it became patently clear what his agenda had been from the very beginning, and why he "chose" me as his victim. I remember the night I met him, he asked me why my previous marriage had ended. I told him that I had caught my husband screwing around and lying about it; that I hated liars and never wanted to be with someone who lied. That was his cue. He knew my weak spot. And his goal was to exploit that any way he could. I had no idea that there was a name to this kind of behavior until 2008. I had always just chalked it up to bad behavior, not realizing that it was a systematic pattern of abuse that was designed to completely destroy me, my financial security, and whatever sanity I had. Everything he did was by design. My two previous husbands had been wealthy and successful. Yes, we had our issues that led to divorce, but it never occurred to me that there were men who preyed on women, who targeted them because of their empathetic nature. The narcissist (or narcopath) looks for people who are kind, trusting, forgiving, successful, diligent, and respected. We were not chosen randomly; we were selected because of what we represented and what they hoped to gain from us. We were especially vulnerable if we had significant assets. And then it's game on.

By the time we were divorced in 2016, I had done hundreds of hours of research into cluster B personality disorders which included sociopathy, narcissistic personality disorder, and psychopathy. I read everything I could get my hands on. I watched YouTube videos by the famous narcissists Sam Vaknin and H.G. Tudor; I read their books, I read books by other victims. I joined a support group. I devoured everything I could to understand what I had been subjected to. I studied his behavior. I watched him, I took note of his lies, his little deceits, his entitled behavior, his undermining of me to my friends, his bold attempts to bolster his position by flat-out lying and pumping himself up to be something he wasn't at all. It has been an interesting journey without which I would not have a trove of material to write about. Every day that goes by, I feel less shattered and hope that one day this will all be nothing but a bad dream.

November 2012 - diary entry
The only way to avoid these episodes is to shut up and never ever dare to express anything that's not praise. Anything less than praise is being taken as an "attack" and he resorts to attacking me! The end result is that no issues are resolved. There is no depth in relating. As long as I am emotionally serving him, fulfilling his needs, capitulating to his wild demands, everything is okay. The bottom line is that I don't matter.

If you are reading this and believe you are the victim of narcissistic abuse, you can take a small amount of comfort in knowing you are not alone. Cluster B personality disorders are on the rise and nobody seems to know or understand why, but the victims are no longer suffering in the shadows as I did for so many years. There are support boards for victims of this abuse that have upwards of 50,000 members. Some of the stories are so horrific that for a victim to read them is a form of re-traumatizing. The lying, stealing, drug use, philandering, deceit, financial abuse as well as physical and mental abuse, cross all socio-economic barriers, and it's not just women who are the victims. Since I joined one support board, three of the women have been murdered by their narcissistic husbands. Two have committed suicide. The stories told by men are every bit as harrowing and display the same patterns. Victims stay with the abuser and stay silent for a variety of reasons – the children, finances, or in my case the complete shattering of my resolve and independence and the ensuing anxiety and depression that make getting through the day the hardest thing you do. And then there is the fear. Fear of what he will do that I hadn't previously thought about; fear for my physical safety; and then the worst fear of all – that I had gone completely insane from this experience. The awareness of Narcissistic Personality Disorder (as well as all Cluster B disorders) has grown in part because of Donald Trump, the world's most notorious narcissist. Do not despair. There is help and support out there. You are not alone.

October 1, 2012 – diary entry

"Amidst all human faults, our innate tendency to self-deceive may be the most dangerous of all." This quote by Alan Townsend hit me between the eyes. It resonated so strongly because over the years I have mastered the art of self-deception, telling myself that surely he must love me a little bit, that perhaps I was just too difficult to live with, and maybe, just maybe, I was imagining he was doing all these devious things. The cloak of self-deception had, for so many years, skewed my vision of reality until I no longer knew what reality was – only the disordered world of living with a narcopath.

October 12, 2012

The tension is so thick you could cut it with a knife. He keeps saying he is leaving but I don't know what he's waiting for.

"I think leaving is really your best option and I certainly wouldn't do anything to change your mind. It doesn't seem that you love me judging by how you've treated me. And you are obviously not happy living here, or anywhere, it seems, and I have to do whatever is necessary to secure my life. For years you told me you hated living in Colorado, and I did everything I could to find a place where we could both be happy, but I have no more options to give you. If you want to leave, you know where the door is."

Instead of implementing a plan, he mopes and pouts. Spends a lot of time on the computer in the other bedroom; sits there hour after hour and never moves unless it's to go into his bedroom and watch TV. I am waiting for him to pack up and go, so I say nothing to set him off thinking that his departure will be imminent. I wanted and desperately needed peace so I walked on those eggshells trying to be invisible and not say anything that could set off another chain of events where he screams and yells at me. After two weeks of this stress, I finally decided if he wasn't leaving then I *was*. I got on Kayak and booked myself a flight to Guatemala. Why Guatemala? I have no idea, other than it seemed like a place where I could lose myself for ten days in Mayan culture, which has always fascinated me. I was still working for the eco-lodge but since most of what I did was online, it didn't matter where I was physically. I found an inexpensive place to stay, and when I had it all set up, I informed him that I was leaving at the end of the month for ten days. I told him that this would give us a good break (and keep me from killing the son of a bitch), and that during this time I hoped he could figure out what it was he wanted to do. As I sat on the plane waiting for it to take off, a sense of relief and peace washed over me that I had not known before. I was going to be free from the abuse for ten days. Free to think and say and do whatever I wanted without being subjected to his tirades, or his criticism and anger. The taxi driver I hired to take me up to Antigua asked me what it was that brought me to Guatemala. My instinctive reply was, "It's cheaper than hiring a defense lawyer to defend me in a murder charge." He just looked at me. Then he laughed. Although my quip was intended to be sarcastic, it was also closer to the truth than anyone knew.

November 2012 – diary entry

The first three days I was in Guatemala, we did not have any contact. It was a cooling off period for both of us. I was having a fabulous time and was so enthralled with Antigua that I could hardly contain myself. I ate in the best restaurants, took a day trip to the mountain town of Chichicastenango where there is a huge Mayan market, spent another day at the hot springs and spa about an hour outside of town where I had every kind of beauty treatment they offered: First a good long soak in the volcano-fed hot pools, followed by a steam bath, a soak in more hot water infused with essential oil, a full body massage, a full body scrub with coffee grounds, and lastly a chocolate body and face mask that was as delicious as it sounds. I felt like a real princess after that. When the taxi driver took me back to Antigua, I went to my favorite restaurant and had a beautiful kale salad topped with strips of sirloin steak, toasted pumpkin seeds, and edible flowers. I felt fortified, relaxed, and pampered. When we finally spoke that evening, I told him about my wonderful experiences, but he never asked any questions or expressed any interest in where I was or what I was seeing, and in fact, sometimes when I shared my experiences, he interrupted me in the middle of a sentence and started talking about something totally different and irrelevant. I gave up. There was no use trying to engage him in anything that I found interesting or fascinating. I spent the remaining four or five days of my trip enjoying my freedom and when we spoke it was only about how the dogs were doing, what the weather was like in Costa Rica, and if there were any issues in the neighborhood I needed to know about. I reverted back to my docile and complacent self if only to keep things on an even keel.

December 31, 2012 – diary entry

The tenants next door moved out one week ago. They never said a word to me – just packed up their stuff and left. I saw a moving truck come and take away their things. I heaved a sigh of relief when I saw them drive away. To their credit, they left the house spotless, which meant I didn't have to hire a cleaning crew to come in. All year I have been collecting the rent, which they pay in dollars. Every month I bundle the money with a little slip of paper indicating the month and year and secure it with a rubber band and then add it to the envelope where I have all the receipts for repairs, etc. The year-end accounting is due to the owner the first week in January, but since we aren't doing anything this New Year's Eve, I decided to crunch the numbers. I dumped the money and dozens of little slips of paper representing expenditures onto the dining room table and got out a notepad. The first thing I do is count the money. Then I added up all the receipts and deducted those expenses from what they paid me. Something wasn't right. I was $800 short. How could that be? Every month they gave me $500 in cash, mostly twenties and tens. But no matter how many times I counted, the end result was still the same. I started to panic. What had happened to that money? It had always been hidden away in the false-bottom drawer of my dresser but for the last couple of months, it had been stashed in a letter holder on the kitchen counter along with some other paperwork. Nobody knew it was there except me. . . and the prince. I got up from the table and stood in the kitchen and stared at him sitting in the corner armchair reading a magazine. Should I say something? He obviously knew I was distressed because I had been sitting at the dining room table swearing and gasping in horror, but he never said a word or even asked what I was upset about. I paced back and forth between the kitchen and the dining room and finally asked him, "Do you know anything about this envelope of rent money that I had stashed on the kitchen counter?"

"Why are you asking me?" He barely looked up from the magazine, and even if he had, he would never have looked directly at me anyway. We almost never made eye contact.

"I'm asking you because $800 is missing, and I've already added up the receipts for expenses, and counted the money that is left and the numbers don't match. So, I have to ask the obvious: did you take any of this money?"

"I'm really sick of your accusatory attitude," he groused, and threw the magazine on the floor. "Fuck you, I didn't steal your money!" And with that, he stomped off to his bedroom, slamming the door.

I had no clue what happened to that money, but there was no way I could not replace it. The owner had trusted me for the last five years to give him an accurate accounting for tax purposes. I was always meticulous about that and even with the fluctuating local currency, my numbers always added up. The only thing I could do was add in $200 a month for the next four months until that discrepancy had been corrected. I didn't even tell the owner. I just quietly took care of it, sent him the account reflecting what should have been there, and left it at that. Happy Fucking New Year!

February 2013 – diary entry

It's been stressful but for some odd reason there have been pockets of calm, which rather than making me feel safe and secure made me even more paranoid. What was he up to that I didn't know about? My birthday is in a few weeks. I know he will forget, as he always does, claiming he thinks it some other date. But the truth is he knows exactly when my birthday is. He chooses to ignore it because he knows it makes me feel devalued and unimportant. Well, I am done with that routine. I had such a great experience in Guatemala that I decided that was where I was going next month to spend my birthday. I quietly made reservations, booked a place to stay, and then a week before my flight, I announced that I was leaving for nine days.

March 2013 – diary entry

I am starting to feel at home in Guatemala. I've met a lot of people who share my interests and background. It seems I have fallen into a routine here and that is comforting to me. I go to the Central Market on market days, take in the sights and sounds, and try to capture the essence of what I was experiencing through photographs. I breathed in the crisp pristine mountain air, ate good food, indulged in the exquisite chocolates, bought beautiful handmade items, and forgot about the stressful life I had left behind in Costa Rica. Since he wasn't really interested in anything I did anyway, I never mentioned the people I met or the lunches and dinners I had with them. Or how I was starting to feel that this was some place I could live. I was beginning to create a new world for myself that didn't include an abusive husband. As I strolled along the cobbled streets and investigated the ruins of churches hundreds of years old, I had no unpleasant memories to mar my experiences. Nor were there things that triggered PTSD flashbacks. I was liberated from all of that, if only for ten days.

When I got back from Guatemala, he seemed unusually friendly and cooperative. Affectionate even. I was starting to think that my going away was actually a good thing for our marriage, and that maybe my absences were a way for him to get his own head straight about the dynamics in this relationship. My flight landed at one-thirty so by the time we got home from the airport, it was almost four o'clock and I was starving. I opened the refrigerator and saw a container of what looked like pasta. I asked him about it and he said it was leftovers from the lunch he had hosted the previous day. A lunch for six people. I didn't think anything of it at the time. I simply warmed up the *fettucine* Alfredo and satisfied my hunger. But later. . . I started thinking. What is it he does while I am gone? This wasn't the first time he had intimated that he had had people over for lunch or dinner. Not that this is a problem, but it made me wonder why he was so eager to do that on his own but never wanted to socialize if I suggested that we invite people to come and eat with us. There was something definitely not right about this, but I didn't put too much energy into analyzing what it meant.

August 12, 2013 – diary entry
    He keeps putting the butcher knife in the dish drainer blade side up. The first time it happened I cut myself reaching in to grab a dish. I assumed that it was an accident so I said nothing that time, nor the third or fourth time, but this time, I was *pissed*. Who leaves a very sharp knife in a dish drainer blade side up? I would've cut myself again had I not noticed the blade.
    "Hey, if you're going to do the dinner dishes, could you please make an effort to put the sharp knives in the dish drainer blade side down?"
    "Why are you asking me that?"
    "Because you insist on doing the dinner dishes and at least a half dozen times the chef's knife is in the drainer sharp side up!"
    Of course, he got all pissed off and we wound up in another screaming row, the thing I swore I would never engage in again. "I can't take any more of your criticism," he yelled at me. "I'm leaving and going back to Colorado. You can stay here in this shitty third world country."
    "Why do you call it criticism if I ask you nicely to please not do something that has the potential to injure me? The fact that I've cut myself because you insist on putting the chef's knife blade side up doesn't matter to you?"

"What the fuck do you want from me? No matter what I do, it's always wrong!"

"Well, yes, putting a knife in that way *is* wrong, and if you ever did that in any of the kitchens you worked in and someone was injured, you'd have been fired, or at least written up and admonished never to do that again. But somehow you think it's okay to do it here and it's not a big deal if I get hurt. Do you just not see how twisted that is?"

"Fuck you. I'm leaving."

Later that day, I did an internet search and found dozens of articles about why putting a knife in the dish drainer blade side up was a very bad idea. I sent him one of the articles. I figured if he saw something written by someone other than me, he would understand that I am not just picking on him, but that it's a matter of kitchen safety. He never said a word. Later, when he started banging and clanging the dishes and pans as he started to wash the dinner dishes, I told him very calmly, "Please just leave them. I will do them later." He stomped off down the hallway and slammed the door to his bedroom, all the while mumbling about how he can't wait to get out of here.

October 2013 – diary entry

I just booked another trip to Guatemala. It has been so tense and stressful that I felt as if I was going to blow apart. As I did the previous times, I booked a flight and made all the arrangements and then informed him that I was leaving. This time he said, "Why don't you ever ask me to go with you?"

"You told me specifically that you had no interest whatsoever in going to either Nicaragua or Guatemala when I brought it up several years ago. In fact, you made it abundantly clear that you had no interest in third world shit holes. I didn't see the point of asking you." Besides, I was thinking, it's the only place where I have no association to my marriage or all the drama I live with on a daily basis. It holds no bad memories or experiences. Why would I want him to come here with me? So he could totally ruin it for me? Antigua has become my sanctuary. The place I go for peace and serenity and an absence of turmoil.

February 15, 2014 – diary entry

He has succeeded in putting this marriage exactly where he wanted it: he can do and say whatever he wants and I live in fear of saying anything at all because of the terror he will unleash on me.

The other night, I was lying on the sofa watching a movie and he goes to the fridge. I hear him very stealthily take the yogurt jar out of the fridge and quietly take the top off. Without even looking, (I didn't have to turn around because I could see his reflection in the computer screen) I said softly and calmly, "If you are drinking out of that jar, please don't; just put it in a bowl," and the next instant I saw him deliberately release the jar from his hand with a flourish and the jar crashed to the floor sending glass and yogurt everywhere. I didn't even react. The intended purpose was to terrorize me. How fucking dare I ask him *not* to do something he wants to do, no matter what my rationale. I was very proud of myself for not reacting; for not saying a word, and just continuing to watch my movie while he griped and groused about the big mess he had to clean up.

April 2014 – diary entry

I stopped talking to him. I haven't engaged in any conversation with him for four days. He's always giving me the silent treatment as a way to punish me, and it's generally recognized as an insidious form of abuse, but two can play this game. The silence is the only thing that keeps me sane. He doesn't understand how much I enjoy that respite from his intimidation and terrorizing tactics. Thinking back to the twenty years of abuse I have suffered, I finally see the pattern. He doesn't give a shit about me, or anyone else. His aim is to be able to do whatever he wants, when he wants, and even if it disrupts our lives or causes friction, it doesn't matter to him.

May 2014 – diary entry

I've been reading his emails because that is the only way I can find out what he is doing behind my back. For the last two years he has been putting the screws to Enzo over the land in Baja. Finally, Enzo told him there was nothing to be done because the seller of the land had changed the terms of the deal and although it was unfortunate, there was nothing he, personally, could do about it. That unleashed a torrent of hideous insults calling Enzo every name in the book and telling him to fuck off. Then I found emails to Paolo about the money I loaned him when I went to Todos Santos in 1997–I don't even remember how much it was– $400 maybe? But he insisted that Paolo has to give *me* back the money I loaned him and if he didn't then he was this, that, or the other thing and to fuck off and never contact him again. I wrote Paolo an email and told him the prince was an asshole and a complete sociopath and that I had never ever mentioned that money because Paolo had assisted me in going to the government offices in La Paz and trying to deal with the seller of the land. I haven't heard back from Paolo. I probably won't. The other night I was lying in bed thinking of all the times he terrorized me and I can't believe it took me so long to figure it out. These things were not isolated incidents but a consistent pattern of psychological torture and abuse. There were times when I was so distressed that I would rather have been dead than live through another one of his tantrums and abuse.

Undated diary entry

Last night I let the dogs out before I went to bed. The chihuahua always has to be leashed or he will take off, even in the dead of night. I walked him to the grassy area between the house and the storage shed but he lurched at a shadow and I tripped on one of the pavers that makes up the walkway. I literally fell flat on my face. I lay there on the wet grass for a minute or two, wondering if I had done any serious damage especially since I landed on my bad knee and hit my face and head on the paving stones. I wanted to cry for help, but instead, I picked myself up and limped quietly into the house and went to the vanity area in my bathroom to see what I looked like. If I had to guess, I'd say I lost *that* fight. There was an abrasion on my cheekbone and a small split near my eyebrow that was bleeding and running down the side of my face. My hand was scraped and I had an abrasion on my forearm. I also had a huge bruise on my knee and shin. I wiped all the blood away, applied antiseptic, put ice to my face, took two Advil, and went to bed. The next morning, he asked what had happened to me and I told him I fell. "Why didn't you call me?"

"I was afraid of waking you up." Afraid that he would yell at me as he had before, afraid that he would be annoyed that I had fallen and now he had to actually do something to help me. I knew better than to think he would take care of me because he had demonstrated so many times in the past that my getting sick, or having surgery, or needing help with anything was just a huge annoyance and inconvenience for him.

ANSWERED PRAYERS

October 27, 2014 – diary entry
This has been a most interesting and blessed week. The owner of the eco-lodge told me that they are changing their strategy and my marketing services are no longer needed. Although I will miss the extra income, I am almost relieved even though that event would set in motion everything that happened after that. At night, when I lay in my bed and before I drifted off to sleep, I prayed. I prayed for forgiveness, prayed for hope, prayed for an answer to the looming problems about the house in Colorado, and prayed for deliverance from this nightmare that had become my life.

I hated who I had become because of all this stress. Prior to meeting the prince, I was always the happiest and most upbeat person I knew. I tried my best to always do the right thing, to do a good job of whatever it was I was doing, to always be positive, and to always give credit where credit was due. People loved working with me because I gave them praise for a job well done and refused to take credit when I could assign that credit to someone else who would benefit more. Twenty years of being abused has turned me into a hateful, spiteful, angry, stressed out, unhappy, mean-spirited bitch. I hated myself for what I had allowed him to do to me. When I looked in the mirror, I often didn't recognize myself. I looked old, tired, sad, worn out, and worn down. In fact, I looked very similar to how his ex-wife looked the night I met her at the restaurant opening. I had a blank look in my eyes. My smile was plastered on my face and didn't look real. My head ached, and I had almost constant pain in my back and neck. I hadn't had a good haircut in years; I had packed on eight unwanted and unsightly pounds on my small frame, but I no longer cared what I looked like. Most days I just pulled my hair into a ponytail and sometimes I went two or three days without showering or even washing my face. I had given up. Depression, hopelessness, and anxiety permeated every cell in my body. Some days I wished I were dead but I was afraid of dying and yet I was already dead. He had killed my spirit and my zest for life. And yet I persevered because I didn't know *how* to really give up. I prayed so hard for a way out of this that would not destroy what was left of my life. I bargained with God; I promised never to have a mean thought or to think ill of someone, just please show me a way to get out of this awful marriage before one or both of us winds up dead.

God responded. And quickly, too!

The loan modification program which reduced the cost of my mortgage on the Colorado house to a manageable amount expires next month. That means that the mortgage is going to go up $350 a month over and above what the current tenant is paying, and which I simply cannot afford to absorb. Especially now that I don't have that extra income from my social media job. The last thing I needed to have happen was to lose that house and whatever equity was still in it. For years, the house had been listed on Zillow so I decided to update it, add some recent photos, and spiff up the selling points. There was also a new function on that site called "Name Your Price" so after looking at comparable cabins in the area, I settled on a figure of $190,000. Before the 2008 crash, the house had been on the market for $275,000 but that was then and this was now, and I had to be realistic. I also needed to make a concerted effort to sell it otherwise it was going to be a tremendous financial burden. I also knew that dumping the house and getting a lump of cash was the only way I was going to be able to end this marriage. There was no way he was leaving without some kind of settlement, and by now, I had resigned myself to that inevitability. Whatever it was going to cost me was still cheaper than that defense lawyer. Imagine my surprise when I opened my email two days later and there was a message from someone in California saying he wanted to buy my house. Yeah, right. I thought it was a joke. I didn't even respond; just deleted the email. Five days later, he sent another email asking if I had gotten the first one and was I really interested in selling because he wanted to buy the house and was ready to pay cash. I sat there for at least a good fifteen minutes staring at his message, wondering if this was some kind of scam. I'd never know unless I investigated. I sent him a reply and said yes, I was interested in selling and the reason I hadn't responded was that I thought it was a joke! He wrote back that it was no joke, he had cash, and was willing to do a quick transaction if we could agree on a price.

When we figured out what we would be saving by not using a realtor, and by splitting any closing costs, we agreed that a ten-grand reduction in the asking price was a fair deal for both of us. There were a few contingencies but basically, he agreed to buy the house "as is" and would assume any responsibility for whatever had to be upgraded, repaired, or maintained. I sat on the sofa in a totally stunned state when I realized that selling the house was going to be my ticket to freedom. After the buyer and I spent several days going back and forth about details, I informed his highness that the house was going to be sold, and that we were aiming for a closing date in January. He had a blank expression on his face, but I knew his devious, sociopathic mind was spinning at warp speed. It only took a couple of days for him to drop the bomb on me: "How much am I going to get out of the proceeds?"

"The money is going to be invested, and besides, it would be ridiculous and foolish for me to give you some part of that money as long as we are still married."

His royalness was less than happy about selling the house, even after I explained to him that unless we did, we would probably lose it because I would not be able to afford to make the payments. Getting a new tenant who could afford to pay the market rental value was going to be a colossal hassle. Selling it was a huge relief. I was out from under the thing that had kept me imprisoned in an abusive marriage and the thing which I fought desperately to hold onto. Meanwhile, the money would be earning interest. Basically, I was waiting for him to make the first move. I figured I would be in a better position if he desperately wanted to leave, so I made no attempt to offer him a settlement. I knew from past experience that it was only a matter of time before he ratcheted up his sociopathic behavior to bring this to a final conclusion. It didn't take long.

Twice this week, he leaped out of the car as we were going someplace. The first time was Tuesday when we were going to do errands. We had barely gotten out of the compound when he started in on how he wanted to get another tree like the big one we planted on the hillside. He kept insisting that it came from someplace it didn't and I kept telling him that it came from the guy who landscaped the walled garden. It wasn't an argument at all; but before I knew it he insisted I stop the car, which I did, and he got out. He whirled around and marched back to the house. I drove off and went to town and did what I had to do. I came home several hours later and he was not talking to me. I figured what he had done was go into my room and rifle through all of the paperwork to figure out how much money I had and where I stashed it. The next day he gave me some line of bullshit about how we shouldn't treat each other that way. "Okay," I said. "Then don't be a goddamn dick." I was done playing his mind games.

Yesterday, Friday, we got into town and he had me so flustered from telling me how to drive, where to turn, how to shift, etc. that I made the wrong turn. He got all pissed off. I said calmly, "I'm sorry, I got confused because you distracted me, always telling me how to drive."

He said, in his usual aggressive tone, "I don't have to put up with this shit," and opened the car door while the car was still moving. My first instinct was to stomp on the gas pedal and throw him into the street where he would, with any fucking luck at all, suffer fatal injuries, but instead I pulled over and stopped. He got out and stormed off. That was at twelve-thirty yesterday and now it's eight o'clock at night. We haven't said a word to each other since. He thinks he is punishing me with the silent treatment, but I've grown to love it and use that time to listen to music (which I know pisses him off) or make phone calls, or watch a movie in peace.

Today, Saturday, I went on the organic farm tour and he stayed home. When I got back in the late afternoon, the door was locked and I couldn't get in so I called him at the neighbor's and he came home and unlocked the door. Then he went into the office and sat there until he went to bed at seven. This is a prelude to what is coming. He is posturing because he knows that the closing on the house is going to happen sometime in the next week or ten days and he is setting up a scenario that will play itself out as I outlined above: he will say he can't take this situation anymore, that he wants to go back to Colorado, that he wants a divorce, and he wants some money. Now I just have to sit and wait and see what his next move is. In the meantime, I am not going to say a word. I am going to carry on as if nothing is wrong, go about my business, and do what has to be done and let him play this out. He is so goddamn predictable it's almost funny. Maybe I should just write the bastard a check and get him the hell out of my life once and for all because it sure as shit isn't ever going to be any different than it's been for twenty years. It's time for the charade to end. It was a lovely day today going to the farm and being with other people and enjoying a peaceful interlude without having to walk on eggshells for fear of pissing him off. He has dominated me and isolated me so that the only time I feel sane is when I am away from him. It's going to be interesting. I just wonder if my predictions will turn out to be true. *Vamos a ver.* We shall see.

February 1, 2015
Whew! The house closing went off without a hitch. I feel as excited right now as I did the day I bought that house. The lawyer we hired was quick and efficient about getting us the documents. The buyer was cordial and polite and we both occasionally remarked what an unusual situation this was – that he was buying a house he hadn't seen from a woman he would never meet, and yet everything was as smooth as silk. We laughed about how easy this transaction had been. Yes, it was a flurry of emails and documents going back and forth, and when the final paperwork had to be notarized at the Embassy in San Jose and then Fed Ex'd to Denver, even that happened without a glitch. The title company officer sent me an email and told me all the docs had been received and processed and she had alerted the buyer to make the wire transfer, which would take place this morning. I checked my bank balance every fifteen minutes to see when it was posted to my account. The second I saw that electronic deposit, I

grabbed my purse and went to the credit union and wrote a check depositing all the proceeds into various CDs in my name only. Finally! I am in charge of my life once again. All I have to focus on now is the final battle of this twenty- year long war of attrition.

I sent the buyer a thank you note and we both laughed at how it was the smoothest transaction either of us had ever done. For me, every transaction I had ever done before I met the prince was like that. My life had been easy and uncomplicated, without entanglements or devious intentions. It confirmed to me that I was not the problem if I could do this and have it all turn out perfectly. Now, I needed time to think and strategize because this was the only chunk of money I was going to have and I could not afford to make any mistakes.

February 15, 2015 – diary entry

Yesterday was Valentine's Day. He had the audacity to wish me happy V Day but I didn't even respond. I dropped him off at the masseur's house and went to do my errands. He called me to pick him up at Eduardo's and then asked if I wanted to meet him to get an ice cream. This is how he tries to lure me back in, but I said, "No, I don't want to do that. I have food in the car. I will pick you up at Eduardo's in ten minutes." We drove home in complete silence. I put the food away and started fixing dinner. He sat on his ass in the computer room and only came out when it was time to eat. Boy, I wish I had his life – he doesn't have to do one damn thing; doesn't have to worry about money, doesn't have to pay bills, taxes, or anything else; doesn't have to deal with bureaucracy; doesn't have to shop or cook or prepare food for the dogs, or even do his laundry. It must be nice.

The only time I feel like myself is when I am far away from him. I did not know that feeling until I got off the plane in Guatemala City the first time and realized that I was FREE

– a whole eleven days of not being screamed at, not being hassled, and not being abused or terrorized. That was really the turning point. Now to figure out how to get him out of here and out of my life for good without it costing me everything I have. And let's not forget that over the years, at least in the beginning of our relationship, he made it very clear to me that he knows how to blow up a house, burn it down, or blow up your car. Thinking back now, I realize that he made these things known to me to instill fear of what he could do if he didn't get his way. What I really find amusing is that he is always talking about learning from his mistakes. That just might be the biggest lie he has ever told. He has no intention of learning anything because as he always reminds me there is nothing wrong with *him* and he likes himself just the way he is.

A recurring nightmare that I have is of waking up and seeing him standing next to my bed. Because the floors are cement and tile, it is entirely possible to not make any sound when walking. And it was for this very reason that I mostly slept with my bedroom door locked. As irrational as it sounds, I always feared that he would sneak into my room and kill me. One night I had forgotten to lock my door and I woke up in the middle of the night and sensed that he was there, bending over near my nightstand.

"What are you doing?" I grumbled from a deep sleep.

"I was just turning out the light which you left on when you went to sleep." That wasn't something that I usually did but I accepted the explanation until I realized much later that what he was really doing was reaching for my handbag which was under my nightstand.

March 2015

With a big chunk of money in the bank, it was time to put on a new roof. We got a bid from the guy who had done all the gates and bars on the windows. He said he could do it next month. The prince insisted that he didn't want me here when it was happening; that it was going to be a big disruption, with lots of noise and activity, and that it would be best if I just went to Guatemala – for two full weeks.

"It's going to take two weeks to put on a new roof?"

"Yes, and I don't want you here when it's being done. Just go to Guatemala and have a good time. I'll stay here and supervise it all."

He was not a bit happy when I asked the contractor to write down how much it was going to cost. Before I left for Antigua, I made sure that amount of money exactly was set aside in an envelope. I suspected that what the prince had planned to do was tell me one number when the real number was much lower and he would pocket the difference. He had done that to other people so I had every reason to be suspicious.

May 5, 2015 – diary entry

What a mistake it was to not record all his bullshit for the last month as it was happening. By the time I left for Guatemala on April 12, we were barely on speaking terms. I was so relieved to get away from him that I could hardly contain myself. Being in La Antigua was like being let out of prison. But when I got home, although things were only slightly less tense, they soon reverted back to how it was before I left – his civility is a thinly disguised patina for the contempt he has for me.

About a week ago I had gone to the store and came back with several sacks of groceries. I didn't think he was home so I gathered all the bags from the car, which were considerable and heavy, and walked to the terrace. There he was holding court with Richard, and several other guys. They were drinking and smoking pot, as usual. He saw me with these heavy bags and never even offered to open the door for me. I didn't say anything in front of his friends, but it did strike me as being rather rude and inconsiderate. In fact, they all basically ignored me. Today, I came back from the market and beeped the horn as a signal for him to come and help me with the packages. Blue, the cattle dog, came out to the driveway barking so I knew he was close by. I beeped the horn again. He came out to the car and in a voice oozing with contempt, said, "I'm eating. You should show some respect."

"I need some help with these packages."

"I told you I was eating. Try being a little more respectful."

"It's you who should show some respect; I'm the one who needs help here." He grabbed one shopping bag and carried it to the door and set it down, while I hauled the rest of the things into the house. Then he went back to eating lunch with his three buddies. I said nothing. Later, while we were getting ready to eat dinner, he mentioned that our neighbors fight a lot.

"How do you know *that*?" I asked him.

"Because sometimes I can hear them."

I jokingly said, "Then he should be nicer to her; everything is in her name."

In a tone of voice I had not heard before, he snarled, "It's fifty-fifty here." The hair on the back of my neck bristled.

"That isn't true. Circumstances change that formula."

"A lawyer told me that laws can mean whatever you want them to mean here," he said smugly.

He is up to something. What lawyer had he been talking to? I had one girlfriend here who was a lawyer but she did only human rights cases. He knew a lawyer who supposedly worked for the cartel. Maybe he asked him? Considering all the lies he tells other people – that he has a big mosaic project in DC, that he has a showing in Atlanta of his mosaics, that he is going to Africa (this he said to the young woman he was stalking on Facebook), failing to mention that he has a wife, I can't but think this is a lie, too. I suspect that he is going to try his damnedest to get half of our financial assets. He has always asked why the house here is in the name of a corporation and wouldn't it be better to have it in my name. He knows damn well the house is untouchable in a divorce if it's in a corporation and he has been trying to guilt trip me and manipulate me into changing that status. It ain't ever going to happen. I have decided to play it out and let him make his move. Eventually, he will have to do something to cause a cataclysmic break-up and that will be just fine with me. It's been years since I thought he might love me even a little bit, but I know now that he doesn't and probably never did; that this was just some fucked up agenda he orchestrated to get what he can out of me. There are some days when I feel so emotionally and physically drained from having to deal with him that I wonder how long I can actually stand it. He's going to Atlanta for a few weeks soon. He wrote to his daughter that he wants to come for a visit because his health isn't so good. I haven't figured out if all this malingering he does is a way to get attention or sympathy, but there is nothing wrong with him that a year or two in a psychiatric hospital wouldn't fix.

There will soon be a showdown but I have resigned myself to having to pay him to go away. The question is how much? He scares me to death because he has made it a point to tell me that he is capable of blowing up a car, burning down a house, cutting brakes on a car, etc. without ever leaving any evidence. I didn't realize it at the time he said those things over the years that it was meant to instill fear in me. And the story about him shooting someone in the knee who had pissed him off? Although I don't believe the story, I believe the intent was to show me that he was capable of doing such a thing and that is why I fear for my life.

PLATA O PLOMO

July 15 – diary entry

It didn't take long for his royal pain-in-the-ass to come up with his plan for how he was going to liberate me of some, if not all, of that money from the sale of the house in Colorado. (Plata o Plomo - money or lead - was Pablo Escobar's motto)

As I was watching a movie the other night, he stood behind the sofa and announced, in that quiet voice that foretells something ominous, "I have a request."

"What is that?" I asked laconically.

"I want half of all the money that is in your account otherwise I am going to the police and have you arrested for lying about that accident."

Well, I'll be damned! I had waited for this day and knew it was coming based on his past history of blackmailing and extorting his other friends. All I could do was laugh. "You're kidding me, right? The statute of limitations expired on that two decades ago. You do realize you just blackmailed me, right? And blackmail is a felony, even in this third world shit hole country, so, fuck *you*!"

He turned on his heels and stormed down the hallway to his bedroom. I waited thirty seconds and then followed him.

"I was wondering how long it was going to take for me to be added to the long list of people you have been blackmailing, extorting, intimidating, and terrorizing. I guess I'm in good company! If you ever threaten me again, I will be the one going to the police!" I walked out of his room and closed the door behind me, and that was the last time we had any kind of conversation for several weeks.

August 2015 – diary entry

We were sitting at the dining room table one night and he grinned at me deviously and boasted, "I'm starting a revolution in Italy. I should be going back there to help with making bombs, and burning down buildings."

I dangled my fork from my fingers and stared blankly at him. "Starting a revolution? You're kidding, right? You're an armchair revolutionary sitting on your ass in Costa Rica, playing on the internet, and I'm just curious – why don't you know how to do something really useful, such as keeping your life together or making honest money?" I got up, put my plate in the sink, and let him sit there by himself to finish his dinner.

The God's honest truth is that I have no goddamn idea who I was married to because he was leading a double life behind my back. It's like waking up from a bad dream and realizing that none of what you based your life on was even remotely true. At times, I felt like those women on *Dateline* who tearfully tell the host that they had no idea their husband was a serial murderer, or rapist, or bank robber.

September 2015 – diary entry

The universe works in strange ways. It's the miracle I was praying for. A mutual friend in Colorado sent him an email and asked him if he would like to come and remodel an old cabin she had just purchased. Of course, he said yes! That's when my plan began to form. I finally had a way out of this mess. He was supposed to go to Colorado in October, so I knew I just had to wait until then to do what I had to do. What I wasn't counting on were the difficulties she was having with the County over certain issues, so there was delay after delay and then it was too cold to do the work so it was decided that spring would be better for him to come. I seethed inside, worried myself sick that something would happen to derail my plan. I didn't see any other way out. There were some days when I didn't think I could tolerate him until March or April, but if I had endured nearly twenty-five years of insanity and abuse, another five months was a drop in the bucket.

Meanwhile, our two dogs were showing visible signs of the stress. One dog was vomiting all the time for no discernible reason. The other dog had chewed all the hair off his backside. My medicine chest looked like a veterinary clinic. I had every kind of pill, ointment, cream, drops, and lotions, but none of them worked for what was plaguing these dogs.

November 2015 – diary entry

I am off to Guatemala again for nine days. This will give me the peace and quiet to sort out all the issues I will have to deal with in the coming months. Guatemala has become my "safe place." He never seems upset that I go either, probably because he has another agenda when I am not here.

December 13, 2015 – diary entry

At nine o'clock I heard him grumbling in the next room. Five minutes later, he came into my bedroom and started bellowing that he needs to go to the hospital and needs the proof of insurance card. I fished the card out of my wallet and handed it to him and asked him what his problem was.

He said he had a bad cramp in his leg. I snickered and asked him what he thought they were going to do in the ER and his response was "give me a shot!" I suggested the he drink some water because I had read recently that dehydration could cause cramping.

His response was "Do you always have to be so critical?"

He got in the car and drove off. A couple of hours later I heard the dogs stir so I went into the living room to find everything dark – no lights on at all – but I saw that he was parked in the driveway. I turned on the living room lamp and went back to bed, and closed and locked my door. This morning when I got up I saw him sitting at the computer and asked him what they did for him at the hospital. He didn't respond. I leaned against the door jamb and asked him again. Without turning around to look at me, he said, "I could've been dying, but they did nothing. That's what we're paying $75 a month for?"

"I don't think having a cramp in your calf can be considered life threatening in any way." When I thought about it, I couldn't even be sure he actually *went* to the hospital. He could easily have gone somewhere else; I had no way of checking.

Last night I was lying in bed, and a wave of terror washed over me like I have never felt before. There is something about him – maybe it's his irrational thought process – that makes me fear for my life. Basically, I am nothing to him, and have never been anything to him, other than someone he could eventually get money out of.

December 15, 2015

That's it! I'm *done*! He's abusive, irascible, moody, secretive, hostile. His phone rings constantly, but he always takes the calls outside, away from the house so I can't hear what he was saying. He does the same thing when he makes a phone call. I know he is up to something, but I have no clue what that is. He still continues to rifle through my belongings. I'm still setting little traps for him – a hair in the door jamb, a piece of paper in a drawer that would fall when opened, photographing the contents of my jewelry drawer so I can compare later to see if anything was moved. It didn't even matter that I lock my bedroom door when I leave the house. He makes sure I know he could get in there by telling me that all he had to do was take a table knife and slide it in the frame and the door opened right up. In total desperation, I sent an email to his daughter. I told her he was out of control; that I couldn't take anymore and she needed to take responsibility for her father. We made arrangements for her to call me on a Saturday morning when she could talk freely. There was no way I could have this conversation in my house so we agreed that I would sit in a local cafe and wait for her phone call. When the phone finally rang, my hands started to shake. We exchanged pleasantries, and then I explained that I was reaching out to her because I was desperate. I gave her some of the highlights of what my life had been like, that he was a compulsive liar, a thief, and was abusive to the point that I was now afraid for my life and also afraid that I could be pushed into doing something that I would later regret. I tried to keep from crying but that was almost impossible. I don't know what I was expecting so it didn't much surprise me when she set out the guidelines.

"Well, to be honest, he had never been much of a father; in fact, he had been a terrible husband and would often disappear for months at a time leaving me and my mother without any money for food. I know he was dealing drugs, using drugs, drinking, and in general being horrible, and as far as I'm concerned, I am only going through the motions of maintaining a father-daughter relationship for the sake of my own child. He was hardly around when I was a little girl and only came into my life as a father about the time you and he met. What he did to me and my mom when I was very young made me determined to never ever be in a position like that again having to worry about money or having food to eat. That is what drove me to be a good student and to excel at my profession. Frankly, Roan, you are his family, not me, and I cannot take any responsibility for him or what he does. I know he makes your life difficult, but I have discussed this with my husband and there is no way he can live *with* us or *near* us. With my high-profile job, I simply cannot afford to have any kind of scandal. I checked around and there is no facility here that could take him. So, the most I could do for you is to take him off your hands twice a year for a month to give you a break." She cried softly as she told me this. I felt sorry for her. She was simply collateral damage in his life of lies, deceit, and crime.

When I thought back to the early days and everything he had said about his ex, I realized that he had been lying about that as well. He had *not* been an exemplary husband and father; he had been that woman's worse nightmare, but at least she didn't stay married to him for twenty years. As she was telling me about her father disappearing for months at a time, I immediately thought about the story her cello teacher told me back in 1992. There were times when her mother didn't have the money to pay for her music lessons and she told the teacher that the prince was missing in action and she had no idea where he was, and asked if she could pay later. Apparently, he told his wife that he was going to Iowa to buy a fancy car for someone and that he would be gone three weeks. Well, three weeks came and went and she hadn't heard a word from him. It wasn't the first time so she didn't panic but when that three weeks had stretched to nearly two months, she called his family in Italy to see if they had heard from him. Imagine her surprise when he came to the phone. When she gave him hell about being in Italy instead of Iowa, his response was "Italy, Iowa, they both start with an 'I' so what's your fucking problem?"

An hour later, our conversation ended and I realized that I was not going to be able to hand him off to his daughter, or any other family member, and therefore, I would have to implement the plan that had been fomenting in my mind ever since I learned he was going to Colorado. The question was *when*? If I didn't plan this out carefully terrible things could happen to me.

December 20, 2015 – diary entry

I was in bed reading last night and he came in and sat on the edge of the bed. "I have something for you," he said. Then he handed me a table knife and said that his friend Steve, for whom he had done work in Colorado, had given it to him.

I stared at it and replied, "That's odd that he would give you just *one* table knife from a silver set. And coincidentally, it's the same silver pattern my mother had." I put the knife in my nightstand drawer and forgot about it.

January 2016 – diary entry

Because I was monitoring his emails, I saw that he had asked his friend in Colorado for traveling money to buy his plane ticket. She agreed and several weeks later, a deposit was made to my account in Colorado and I started searching for a ticket. It was all set! He was leaving April 12. I just had to hang on until then.

February 12, 2016

I want my life back – the life I had before he moved into my house in Colorado and made a complete shamble of everything. He is a disgusting, amoral asshole. And his daughter confirmed that he has always been this way, so I know it isn't about me – this is just how he has gone through life thinking anything he wants is there for his taking and he will oft cite that biblical phrase "God helps those who help themselves." I'm counting the days until he leaves. My survival depends on my keeping it together until then. Once he leaves, I can make my move.

I used to be so happy – always looked forward to every day, always found something good or funny in every situation, always had a lot of friends, an active social life, and loved to travel. Twenty-five years of being emotionally manipulated and abused has left me barely able to function because I am wrapped in fear and anxiety most of the time. To say that I hate him would be an understatement. I wanted a divorce in 1999 but then he had that accident and here we are. Thank God, I have managed to wrestle any financial exposure away from him. My greatest fear was that he would get himself in trouble and I would have to foot the bill or he would cause me to lose everything I had because of his bullshit. Well, that can't happen now because his name isn't on anything – not the house, not the car, not the bank accounts, not the electric bill, phone bill, or the water bill – and I've even changed the beneficiaries on my bank accounts because he's not getting one dime of my money.

February 18 – diary entry

Took my cattle dog to the vet. He has licked himself bald on his hips and it was bleeding. Dr. David took blood, did a skin test, gave him a medicated bath, and gave me a bill for $120. He'd ruled out parasites, heart worms, Ehrlichia, and a half dozen other things dogs are susceptible to in the tropics just as he had done four or five months ago, so it could only be stress. Poor dog.

Anytime the prince gets too close to me, the dog gets between us and growls and barks. He clearly doesn't want this man anywhere near me and I think if he tried to strike me, the dog would attack him.

February 25

Last Friday when Helga and I were coming back from the market we saw a mangy dog near entrance to the development. The next day the dog was in our yard looking for food and water. I left a handful of food on the side of the house, which she found and ate. Sunday, the dog showed up on the terrace again and of course the prince was yelling at me to get rid of it, and the dogs were barking ferociously at her until she cowered in a corner near the garden door. My heart just broke at that moment to see something so fearful. She reminded me of me!

I took her next door to the vacant house and gave her some water and more food while we tried to figure out what to do with her. Monday morning, I took her to the vet – she has mange and some infected areas, but the vet gave me all the medicine and I brought her back and settled her in at the vacant house next door, which has an enclosed yard. Meanwhile, I called and wrote everyone asking for help finding a home for this dog. All this week she's been there and I've been going two or three times a day to feed her and play with her.

The prince announced after I came back from feeding her, "If I had my way, I'd take her out to the highway and dump her."

My heart froze because I know if I don't find her a home before I go to Guatemala next Thursday, he might just do that. What kind of person does that? Oh, yeah, fucking sociopaths who have no empathy for anyone or anything. I really feel like kicking his ass out and keeping the dog. It would be a better choice.

All day today I felt as though I were going to implode. My breathing is rapid, my pulse rate is up, and my head is pounding. I don't know how much more of this I can take. I thought I could stick it out until he went to Colorado the middle of April but then tonight, he made some comment about he wasn't sure if he was going and I nearly dropped whatever was in my hands. If he doesn't go, I don't know what the hell I am going to do. My plan was to get him out of here peacefully, and then tell him he couldn't come back; that it was over, and I never wanted to see him or talk to him again. But if he doesn't go on his own, how am I going to get rid of him? It will be an awful, horrible scene and to be quite honest, I would rather be dead than go through that yet another time. It could also escalate into violence.

Although I can't remember exactly what we were fussing about, he said, "We don't have any children. Let's just end this now."

"For fuck sake, you've been saying that for twenty plus years and you haven't left yet. JUST GO!" But for that goddamn accident he had and then everything he put me through after that, I'd have divorced him in 1999.

Later this afternoon, he says to me, "I'm out of pot. Can you give me a little bud?"

"Well, that's real cheeky of you after you took my stash – yet again. Maybe you ought to smoke less! I'm just curious – how did you ever get the idea that rummaging through peoples things and taking their stuff was okay?"

"Just be quiet about that."

"No, I *won't* be quiet about that because every time you do it, it's a form of mental rape."

"I went all the way to Colorado and packed up your stuff so now you have everything here. I don't know what you are complaining about after I did that for you."

"You are comparing apples and oranges. Doing that task does not give you permission to take my things. Maybe you need to work on your impulse control." Some days I just want to lie in bed and cry until I can't cry anymore, but I am afraid to. I'm afraid of what he will do to see me so vulnerable. So I hold it all inside until I am ready to explode. Which is how I feel right now – that I am only a hair's breadth away from a complete breakdown from which I might never recover. That's what scares me so I just pretend that I am carrying on as best I can, when in reality my grip on reality is tenuous at best.

February 27, 2016 - diary entry

He informed me that his daughter was coming down for a vacation along with friends and that we were invited to tag along. I told him I had no interest in doing that, but he was free to participate. He said the least I could do was come down to the beach for the weekend before they went to other locations. I told him I would think about it while I was in Guatemala where I was going to spend my birthday, as I had done for the previous three years.

In all the time we were together, he only ever remembered my birthday once or twice and that was only because I had dropped a huge hint a few days before. Narcissists and sociopaths do this because it is designed to make the person feel unloved, unappreciated, and unimportant. And that was exactly how it made me feel the first fifteen times he forgot. Then it just got easier to go away so I didn't stew about him having forgotten. I knew on this trip that I had a lot of details to work out in my head about how I was going to implement "The End." It is time for me to gather my strength and resolve because with the proceeds of the house safe in the bank, I now have the means to make the changes I need to make if I am going to survive.

March 2016 – diary entry

Today is my birthday and I am spending this week in Guatemala as I have done for the previous three years. The first thing I did after pouring myself a cup of coffee was to look at the calendar and count how many days I have to deal with him once I return home – thirty-six days, and I would silently tick them off in my head as his departure date approaches. Exactly ten years ago today, I was sitting in the restaurant of an exclusive resort having dinner with two girlfriends. I announced at dinner that never again would I celebrate a birthday and still have to deal with his ongoing abuse. I said the exact same thing ten years before that. But circumstances being what they were, it just wasn't possible to extricate myself until all the pieces were in place. Twenty years of my life had slipped through my fingers. I can't get those years back. To celebrate my upcoming freedom, I took a shuttle to the mountain town of Chichicastenango to see the large Mayan market where hopefully I find myself the perfect birthday gift.

April 4 – diary entry

His daughter arrives tomorrow with her husband and child, and two other couples and their children. They have an itinerary planned so the only time we will get to see them is when we go to the beach and stay in the hotel next to the big house they rented. But as usual, there was always a major dust-up.

Yesterday, he moved the pizza oven he built from the little garage he was using as a workshop to the restaurant on the main highway. I expressed concern about whether it was safe to be left out all night and didn't he worry about vandalism or theft? He said they had cameras on the oven, and the cops hang out there all night. I said, "If the cops have to go on a call, they won't be there the entire time. . ."

He exploded in a rage, "WHAT THE FUCK DO YOU WANT FROM ME?"

I said, "Only for the oven to be safe; after all, I've got some investment in it too now."

"Fuck you, bitch!"

"Get. Out. Of. My. House! You will *not* talk to me like that. I'm sick of this abuse." He had waved a red cape at an angry bull! I was livid!

"You're going to throw a sixty-nine-year-old man out on the street?"

"Yes!

"You can't do that!"

"I *can* and I *will*. I am sick of the abuse."

"Forty-five percent of this house is mine."

"I don't know where you got that idea because the house is owned by a corporation. Even I don't own the house. You need to leave. You need to just go away and leave me alone. I can call the cops and have you thrown out of here."

"Go ahead! Call them!" he taunted.

I reached for the phone and thought, oh great, there'll be a nasty scene and all the neighbors gossiping about it, so I put the phone down.

Then his face contorted in rage and he started screaming, "You're a fucking bitch!"

That *did it*! I doubled up my fist and lunged at him from across the room and slugged him in the shoulder as hard as I could. He stepped back and called me a fucking bitch again plus a few other things, so I slugged him again. I was in a blind rage and only by the grace of God did I not grab a knife and stab him. I wanted to kill him. At that moment, I realized only one of us was getting out of this marriage alive. April 12 could not come soon enough. Before things really got out of hand, I went to my bedroom and locked the door. I spent the rest of the day in bed. What upset me more than anything was that I had taken the bait. He had deliberately provoked me into the worst reaction to make me look like the crazy one. Try as I might to not react, there were times when his verbal and mental abuse was just too much and my reaction was typical of someone suffering from Complex PTSD. I just wanted the abuse to *stop*!

The next day he left to meet up with his daughter and her friends. I was supposed to join them but I made up an excuse to put it off for another day. A sick dog was the perfect excuse. I got to the beach two days later; we weren't talking. It must have been obvious but I didn't care. I stayed as far away from him as I could, ticking off the days in my head until he was leaving. On the two-hour drive home, we said not one word. I kept my distance after that, too, only speaking to him if it was absolutely necessary.

April 11, 2016

"How am I going to get to the airport tomorrow?

"Take a taxi or take the bus. I'm not getting up at that hour. Sorry."

Our neighbor, who is usually up at that time, agreed to take him to the bus station. I went to sleep knowing that this was the last day I would ever have to put up with his sociopathic abuse. I slept well for the first time in months.

April 12 – diary entry

Hallefuckingluja! He's GONE! I almost can't believe it. I am alone. I am in peace. I woke up this morning to an eerie quiet about the house. It was as though a thousand-pound weight was lifted from my shoulders. My day of liberation arrived.

I spent the day trying to sort out how I was going to implement my plan, and after I did some quiet meditation it all unfolded to me as I knew it would. I went into the storage shed and gathered up all the empty plastic bins and started packing his stuff. I gathered up some of his tools, and stacked them on the terrace. This was not going to be an easy task given how much stuff he had and how I had to go through it to make sure he didn't have any of my things.

Then I looked around the house. Most of his things were confined to his bedroom, which smelled like a locker room or a bull pen. I opened the window and lit some incense, then took an inventory. I took a deep breath and started emptying his drawers. I piled his clothes on the bed and then put them in plastic bins and moved them to the terrace. With each bin that I filled, I realized that I was that much closer to ending this twenty-five year-long nightmare.

Two days later he called. His voice was all soft and velvety, as though nothing was going on in the background of our marriage. It's the voice he always used when he was hoovering me in an attempt to create another golden honeymoon period. This time I didn't take the bait. He said, "Looks like this project is going to be quicker than I thought and I should be back in a couple of weeks, rather than the two months I originally estimated."

I gasped and fell silent.

"Are you there? Hello?"

"Yes, I'm here, but I have something to tell you. I am packing up all your things and putting them in bins, which I am stacking on the terrace. You can no longer live in my house. My suggestion is that you stay there and let me ship your things to you."

"WHAT?" he shrieked. "Why are you doing this? What is going on in that head of yours?"

"It's very simple. I can no longer live with someone I want to kill. You have abused me for two decades, and I am *through*! This is *over*!"

"I never thought you would do this to me. But there are issues we need to sort out so I am not going away without a fight."

"Fine. Our lawyers can work out the details. I have nothing more to say to you." And with a sense of peace and calm, I hung up the phone.

I sent his daughter an email and told her to tell him to stay there, that this was over, and I could not endure one more incident of abuse. That's when she told me she had already gotten him a ticket to return here on April 28. My lawyer told me to not let him into the house because that would open up an adverse possession situation and I sure didn't want that.

April 29, 2016

For two weeks all I did was clean. His bathroom was disgustingly dirty. There was so much soap scum on the glass tiles and window that it took me more than a week of hard scrubbing to get most – but not all – of it off. Then came the kitchen – which had become so disorganized over the years that it was an almost insurmountable task. I hired the neighbor girl to come and clean out and organize the kitchen drawers and cupboards. I realized very quickly that this was not a one or two-day project but rather would take weeks, maybe a month or two, to completely organize this house. It was chaos wherever I looked. But to really accomplish the big purge, he needed to get the remaining stuff out of his bedroom.

He arrived in country yesterday and spent that night at a friend's B&B near the airport. I told him in a previous phone conversation that no way in hell was he going to spend another night in my house, but I would find him a place to stay for four or five days until he figured out what he was going to do. I went to the local hostel and paid for four nights. He called and said he would like to come to the house to get some of his things, and to finish packing what was left in his bedroom. I told him he would have exactly one hour to do that and then he would have to leave.

He showed up in a taxi an hour later, walked into the house and went directly to his bedroom. He kept saying over and over, "I can't believe you are doing this," as though he had no fucking clue why. Then he started hounding me about taking our chihuahua with him. I told him that was not going to happen; that he was staying in a hostel where dogs aren't allowed. He had barely been here thirty minutes when he announced that he had done all he could do and would I take him back to town. I tried to keep the conversation to a minimum, neutral and civil, but as usual, he started ranting about all the crime in this country and I quietly said that there is crime everywhere. In a very firm, but menacing voice, he said, "But in this country, I can hire a hit man for $100." My blood froze. I took it as a veiled threat.

I dropped him off at the hostel, and told him to please decide when he was coming for the rest of his belongings. He said he would call me in a day or two.

Two days later, he called. He claims to have something wrong with his leg and couldn't walk. I told him to go to the clinic and see a doctor. Instead of going to our health service clinics he went to a private orthopedist and called me from there. "WHAT SHOULD I DO?" he bellowed.

Exasperated with yet another complaint or ailment, I yelled back, "WHY ARE YOU CALLING ME? You're at the doctor. Talk to him." I haven't heard from him since and that doesn't bode well. It's three-thirty on Sunday and haven't heard a peep. His words in the car the other day that life is cheap in Latin America and for a hundred bucks you could have someone killed, resonated in my head.

He called and asked if I would pick him up in town and bring him to the house so he could finish getting his things. He said to pick him up on the corner near the liquor store on the back road. I got there a few minutes early and parked. I sat and waited. A few minutes later, I saw an old man coming down the street, walking with a slight limp. It wasn't until he got twenty feet from the car that I realized it was the prince. He looked old, shriveled, and broken down. He radiated misery and defeat, as if his entire past life had finally caught up with him. What surprised me the most was that I felt nothing for him except pity. I couldn't even feel rage towards him, and I realized for the first time that he was a complete stranger to me. Someone I had spent twenty-five years with and didn't know at all. We drove back to the house in complete silence. He went through some things in the storage shed and then left.

May 5, 2016

I did not hear from him today or yesterday at all, but he came on Monday after not contacting me all weekend. I read some of the emails he was sending people, full of lies and crazy accusations. The funniest one was that I had become a lesbian and wanted to get rid of him so I could have female orgy parties in his bed. That made me laugh. The rest of his accusations didn't even make sense. He was babbling incoherently to almost everyone. The smear campaign, for which sociopaths are notorious, had begun. I downloaded or cut and pasted all of the messages into a file. I knew I might need them at a later date to prove how insane he really was. This was no ordinary smear campaign – it was a scorched earth endeavor. A narcopath will never admit that a break-up is their fault and will immediately engage in a systematic campaign of lies, character assassination, malicious gossip, backstabbing with totally baseless and cruel insinuation, and using projection (accusing the victim of what they themselves are doing). These things are a major indicator of personality disorders, and he was displaying his disorder with flying colors!

He showed up in a taxi, spent about an hour packing up the rest of the stuff in his room, moved everything onto the deck and said he'd be back the next day to move everything. I did not hear from him Tuesday, Wednesday, and now Thursday. I am sure he is playing some game, but I am not biting. I know he thinks he is going to get half my house but that will never happen after I spoke to my lawyer. The money in the credit union is exempt from third parties so I think I am safe there, but this bastard is so evil and wicked, there is really no way I can anticipate the kind of fuckery he will try to pull.

The dogs are so completely different now with just me that it's mind boggling. I can only imagine what they must have been feeling to have this monster screaming at me all the time. When he came on Monday, the cattle dog growled at him and wasn't really sure if he should let him in. But then he always growled and barked whenever the prince got anywhere near me.

In the midst of my cleaning frenzy, I found something of mine in his room and put it in the drawer of my nightstand where I found the knife he had given me. I went to the dining room and pulled out the wooden box that held my mother's silver. Wouldn't you know it, there were only five knives, and six of every other spoon and fork. But more distressing than the fact that he gave me the knife and said it came from someone else, was that *six* place settings were missing. Did he steal those too? Of course, he did, along with other silver forks, knives, and spoons that his friend supposedly "gave" him, which I never believed for one second.

Two days later – diary entry

There is never a dull moment. In the midst of all this chaos, I decided to see the dermatologist about the bump on my forehead. It had grown to the size of a dime and didn't look particularly strange, but it shouldn't be there and was starting to give me cause for concern. The doctor was nice enough. He looked at the bump, which I figured could be removed with liquid nitrogen spray. He asked if I had other spots on my body, which I did. He zapped those. Then he asked me to sit down in the chair across from his desk. Pointing to the bump under the strand of hair that had fallen onto my forehead, I said, "But you didn't remove the spot on my face that I came here about."

He looked at me with kind, but sad, eyes. "That is cancer."

I don't remember if I heard what he said after that. The room was spinning, my heart was pounding, and I thought I would pass out. The doc sensed my distress and told me to take a deep breath then explained that he thought removing it in an in-office procedure would take care of it and I probably wouldn't need any chemo or radiation if the margins were clear. I must have agreed with him because I walked out of the office with an appointment for five days later. I went home and collapsed on the bed. How could this be happening to me now, just as I was about to take control of my life? Was I going to need chemo; was I going to die? It was almost too much to process, and I felt completely overwhelmed. I finally fully grasped the meaning of this phrase: When you are going through hell, don't STOP!

The procedure took about forty-five minutes. With enough Novocain, I didn't feel a thing, not even the sixteen stitches it took to close up the five-inch incision. I went home and went straight to bed and lay there, motionless. The doc told me in very explicit terms that I was to have no stress; that I must rest, eat well, stay calm, take the antibiotics, and put the cream on the incision twice a day. He assured me I should be fine but he couldn't be certain until the pathology report came back. Oh, no stress? Was he kidding? I was about to enter a vortex of stress that had no end in sight. I sent the prince a Facebook message telling him about the cancer surgery and how I needed peace and quiet to recuperate. I sent him a picture of the incision so he'd know I wasn't making it up.

Several hours later I received a reply that said, "At least you have a home to recuperate in." Short and sweet.

Later same day

I am starting to freak. His silence is deafening. It could only mean two things: he is plotting and scheming, or he really has gotten so depressed that he may do something to himself, which wouldn't necessarily be a bad thing. I tried to be pleasant when he was here on Monday. I made breakfast and offered him some. He wouldn't eat, nor would he even have a cup of coffee. He came in and out of the house with that blank, soulless look he gets that is very scary. I gave him $1100 so he could either rent a place to live or continue to pay for the hostel. I checked his email to see if I could glean what he was up to. There was a pathetic email to his daughter claiming he's been sleeping in the park, (a total fabrication!) that his soul is dead, he's terribly depressed, blah blah blah. She told him she bought him a ticket back to Colorado, that things would get better, and to just hang in there until he could leave on May 24. Several days later two people showed up in an SUV and said they were there to take all the things that belonged to him. It took several trips but within two hours, everything was gone, and I was FREE!! Or so I thought.

Then the threatening emails started coming: How he was not going to go away quietly, how he wanted half of everything, including this house, how he needed to be compensated for any work he did on the Colorado house, etc. And the things he was telling other people were completely insane: besides the lesbian story, he was telling everyone how I had hundreds of thousands of dollars and he was going to get half of that. The funny part was that on Monday he claimed I had $130,000 in the bank, by Wednesday it had grown to $175,000, and by Saturday, to whoever he was bullshitting, the sum had soared to $190,000, and how I was making $2000 a month in interest on that money. With each email I read, he sounded crazier and crazier, and then a wave of fear went through my body. A $100 hit man, cutting brake lines, making bombs, blowing up houses, burning down houses. I realized that I was in danger.

The next morning, I went with a neighbor (who already had a restraining order against him for a variety of infractions) to the court house and swore out a complaint and asked for an order of protection, fearing that my life could be in danger. I enumerated all the reasons why I thought that and stated in the declaration that "this had never been a marriage; it was a hostage situation." Serving him with the papers was going to be a difficult task since he was lying to everyone about where he was staying. The cops couldn't find him, but they were on the look-out should he come anywhere near my house.

Several days later, I got in my car, turned the ignition, and heard a faint crackling noise. I flew out of that car so fast, sprinted down the fifty-foot terrace, and crouched down on my hands and knees with my hands covering my head and waited for the explosion. After two or three minutes with no big boom, I got up and walked back to the car, took the key out of the ignition, and slammed the door. I wasn't going anywhere. The only place I felt safe was inside my house. There were still ten days before he was scheduled to fly back to the US, so I just had to bide my time. However, three days later I realized that I had to go buy food for me and the dogs. I figured I could go to town, grab what I needed and be home within an hour. I decided to go to the next town, which was only five miles farther away to shop at the new market. There was almost no chance that I would run into him there. As I was driving on the two-lane freeway, I saw in my rear-view mirror a motorcycle approaching my car. Both the passenger and the driver were wearing black helmets that covered their faces. The recent news stories about several people being assassinated while in their cars by hit men on motorcycles flashed into my head. "OH MY GOD!" I screamed as they pulled up alongside my car. This was IT! They were going to kill me. I was sure that I was going to pass out. But then they took off like a rocket and pulled in front of me and soon were out of sight. I had to find someplace to pull off the road and just sit there until I regained my composure. I made a very quick stop at a grocery store and went immediately home and stayed put.

I didn't think I was at all paranoid either, especially when I read this post on my narcissistic abuse support group: "He called saying he wanted to get back together with me. Boy was I gullible. While I was in his truck driving around talking about what I thought was our future together, someone he hired rigged my vehicle. As I drove away from him, I noticed he followed. Next thing I knew my passenger wheel came off and I was in the air. I hit two trees and my car flipped four times at speeds gaining up to 90 miles an hour. I broke so many bones. Was paralyzed for a time being. While in the hospital (he thought I was dead) he went to our house and cleared it out the next day and emptied all the bank accounts. He turned off the water and heat in my home, so when I did get home, I couldn't take care of myself or my children. This man divorced me and launched a smear campaign that made me the bad guy I'm sharing my story because there were signs from the beginning in our five-year relationship. He lied all the time. He made threats . . . ."

I did not want to wind up like that woman. The consensus among other narcissistic abuse survivors is that when you break up with the narcopath, they suffer a narcissistic injury and unleash a rage on like you have never seen before. Knowing this, I became ever so cautious in my dealings with him. The last thing I wanted to do was incite his anger, which always lurked just beneath the surface. Besides, we were long past the point of arguing about anything. This marriage was over. I just wanted to survive the break-up.

May 23, 2016 – diary entry

I agreed to meet him at one of the places he said he was staying to get the SIM card back for my cell phone. He walked out of the apartment house dressed to the nines. I waited in my car across the street. When I rolled down the window, he shoved the phone in my face and said, "Why did you put this picture of my dog on here?" There was an adorable picture of the rescued chihuahua.

I told him I hadn't done that because I hadn't had access to his phone! Then he demanded that I give him the dog, which I said I wouldn't do. He started crying. My patience for his theatrics had run out, but I kept calm. "Please just give me the SIM card."

He handed it to me and made more veiled threats and said, "I'll see you in court. You are NOT going to get away with this!"

"Oh, shut the fuck up!" I replied and sped off. I didn't want to waste another ounce of energy on him. He was leaving tomorrow and this nightmare would be on its way to an end.

May 24, 2016 – diary entry

I woke up at my normal time, around five forty-five, made coffee, and while it was brewing opened a flight status app and searched for his Denver flight. It said departure would be on time at 7:05 AM. I updated the information every few minutes until I saw that the plane had taken off and then burst into tears and started shaking. I felt nauseous, elated, scared, thrilled, happy, sad, devastated and relieved – all at the same time. I went back to bed and I stayed there for the entire day. I was completely enervated and barely had the energy to lift my head from the pillow. The siege was over! He may have left the country and was technically out of my life, but the wreckage he'd left behind still had to be cleaned up. And I was the biggest piece of wreckage. Later that night, after I had tried to pull myself together to eat something, I started blocking him everywhere I could – Facebook, email, telephone, Skype, but alas I was not able to block him on Magic Jack.

June 1, 2016 – diary entry

I am in the spin cycle. I knew I had to keep busy, stay grounded, and not get caught up in the maelstrom that he was going to create. The first thing I thought of was my book – the book that had been languishing on Amazon for over a decade and a half. I called the publisher and asked about how to turn it into an e-book. We talked about my options and the costs, and I decided to go for it. The publishing rep sent me a pdf copy of the original manuscript and I started editing. My goal was to knock off fifty to seventy-five pages, make some revisions on the cover graphics, and have it out in e-book form by the end of the year. This project would keep me focused on something positive as I waited for the divorce to become final. There were still a lot of projects to do on the house, so it's going to be very busy for the next five to six months.

EXPOSED

June 28, 2016 - diary entry

Well, this has been an interesting week. A friend of mine in Colorado contacted me and when I told her that he was back in town and that we were getting a divorce, she said, "I never could understand what you were doing with him. He is such a creep." When I asked her some questions, she told me that he had gotten busted shoplifting at the charity thrift store, and was now banned from ever going in there. She also said that he broke into her house several times and stole money and pot, eagle feathers, and a few other items. When I told that story to three different friends, they all asked if it was possible that he was the one who burgled the house next door (which I was managing) while the occupants were on vacation in the US. I got the blame, was ostracized in my own neighborhood, was called names, and when I started thinking back to the incident, it could only have been him who went in their house. Basically, he threw me under the bus and let me take the blame and the ridicule. I remember how outraged he was when I was accused, but in retrospect, he was just happy to have me blamed which deflected any suspicion away from him.

Speaking of burglaries: In our development there had been multiple incidents where our neighbors' houses were completely cleaned out. Two of them more than once, and when I say "cleaned out" I am talking the furniture, interior doors, appliances, and even the toilets. One of these neighbors came to me and expressed his concern that there was a possibility that the prince was behind some, if not all, of these incidents. I nearly vomited when he said that, but then he went on to explain why his suspicions had validity. Their house was unoccupied at least six months of the year because they lived in France. After the second burglary Louis had installed a complicated and sophisticated alarm system, and the day he was installing it, his highness was there asking questions – where did this wire go, what is this one for, what happens if this one is cut, etc. At the time, Louis assumed that the prince was a friend, or at least a good neighbor, so he explained to him how it would be impossible for someone to bypass this new system from the outside because they wouldn't know how it had been set up. In the first burglary, the thieves even managed to get into the lower level of the house where the car was stored in the garage and took the tires, the battery, and then broke into the secure room where all of Louis's tools were stored. It had cost Louis and his wife Sara approximately $4000 to replace everything that had been stolen, and in the second burglary, they had stolen the washer and dryer, some of the interior doors, and had unscrewed the toilets but left them behind. They were determined to not have it happen a third time. This new system was going to prevent that. The following week Louis and Sara returned to Paris. Ten days later, their house was broken into in the middle of the night and cleaned out once again of all the new items they had purchased to replace what been stolen the first time and second time. The system Louis installed had been completely bypassed, so the alarm never went off and the thieves worked throughout the night. As Louis was telling me all of this in broken French and English, the world around me was starting to swirl. I had to interrupt him mid-sentence and run into my house to lie down. Now things were starting to make sense – how the neighbors behind me had their storage shed burglarized the night before they were moving out of their house. The date of their departure was the best kept secret in the neighborhood. Even I did not know the exact date, but the prince did. And it didn't take long before other neighbors made the connection. Nobody said anything to me until after he had left the neighborhood. Then there was rampant speculation as to just how many of the twenty-five burglaries we had had here over the years had he been involved in. I couldn't process any of this. Was it possible that he had orchestrated these burglaries?

I had so many revelations while I was sleeping and one of them was about the missing $800 from the rent money for the house next door while I was the manager. Anyone who knows me knows I don't misplace, misappropriate, or lose $800. There is no doubt now that he stole that money. He knew where I kept it, each month's rent in cash secured by a rubber band and a little note that said which month it was for. I was meticulous about my record keeping. When I discovered that the money was missing, I asked him then if he had taken it, and in his usual fashion of righteous indignation, he denied it and was upset that I would even think to accuse him. But when I confronted him a second time it in the "last letter" he didn't deny it. This would explain, in part, why he was always pressuring me to sell the house and move away. "Too many robberies," he would whine. "We're on their target list," he insisted. "We need to move somewhere else," he implored. I think the real reason he wanted to move was that he knew eventually people would figure out that he was masterminding these events.

Just down the road from our development was where a gang of thieves hung out in front of a ramshackle store/bar. They were there almost every day, loitering. Young, able bodied men, who should've had jobs. Almost every time the prince and I went to town and passed them standing in front of the store, his would give them some kind of hand signal. Finally, I asked him, "What the fuck are you doing waving at those guys? Are you letting them know that our house is unoccupied? How do you even *know* these guys?" As usual, he dismissed my questions with a wave of his hand. I called a friend and had iron gates installed on all the doors, a cross bar on the upper windows that opened, and had the alarm system beefed up and signed on with a security company to give us extra protection when we were at home and especially when we were away from the house. He was upset that I had spent the money to do this but I couldn't live in the fear anymore. But what was ironic was that I was trying to protect myself from outside forces, when the thief was living with me. Even the local police had their suspicions. Like the pyromaniac who shows up at the fire he set, the prince was always the first one to arrive at the burgled house when the police got there. He had a long list of scenarios as to who was behind these incidents. Because there had been so many burglaries, the local police were patrolling our neighborhood ten times a day. After the prince went back to the US, there were no burglaries, and there have been no burglaries in the two years since he's been gone. This fact was not lost on the local police.

July 2016 – diary entry

I got an email from his daughter who now wants to talk about a settlement, and when I'm done telling her who her father is I'm going to conclude with "he aint't getting one more dollar out of me after giving me $100,000 in debt I didn't have before I married him."

August 7, 2016 – diary entry
The last couple of weeks have been so stressful that it's all I can do to stay grounded. I started having nightmares again and would often wake up crying or yelping and then not be able to go back to sleep. The divorce is in process – his daughter has sent me all the documents that I had to print out, sign, and have notarized. The settlement agreement is as we discussed – he gets a sum to be paid in two payments – the first one when he has signed the settlement agreement and the divorce is filed – and the second when the divorce is final. We also signed papers saying we wanted a divorce without having to appear in court. It should be a slam dunk, but I'm still nervous. The most interesting thing about the financial statement his daughter filled out was that he claimed to have not worked one single day since his accident in 1999. She hand-wrote this statement, obviously at his direction, but what she doesn't realize is that he did that for a specific reason. He knows it was a lie because he worked part-time for most of the time, except for the last five years. He had her lie about something and later when she doesn't meet his demands, he will blackmail and extort her. The poor woman has no idea what is coming down the trail for her. It won't matter that she is his daughter or that his actions could have a negative effect on her life and career as a lawyer. Everyone, even children, are objects to be used and exploited.

One of the most disturbing revelations I had was waking up and thinking about the two carat cabochon emerald ring he asked me to sell for him right after I met him. At the time his reason for giving it to me was that it was an item that could be sold easily in Beverly Hills. I had not thought of that ring in more than twenty years, but when I awoke in a cold sweat, it dawned on me that the reason he wanted *me* to sell it was that he had stolen it and couldn't be attached to it by pawning it in anywhere in Colorado. It is the only thing that makes any sense. I barely knew this guy, and he was having me fence stolen property. Who else did he steal from? What else did he steal? I don't even want to know. But there was more to come.

Undated diary entry

The other day one of his old buddies in Denver called looking for him. I told him I had no idea where he was, nor did I care, but I hoped he was dead. Charles wanted to know what had happened that made me so angry, so I told him an abbreviated version of the last ten years of our marriage. There was dead silence on the other end. Then Charles cleared his throat and said, "Boy, that's quite the saga, but didn't you *know* he was a thief?"

"No, I didn't, and what exactly do you mean?"

"Well, he started out stealing dogs from rich people in Milan and holding them for ransom. He was quite the famous dog thief back in those days."

Was I hallucinating?

"Then he started stealing other things; it was a natural progression."

"And was there a good reason why you or any of his other old pals didn't tell me this?"

"We all thought you knew and just didn't care. He was involved in a lot of illegal activities."

"Yes, he told me about the drug smuggling and the false bottom suitcases."

"I think he even got his old father involved when he sent him a false-bottom suitcase filled with hashish and the police paid a visit to his father's country house demanding an explanation."

"He's a shameless monster, Charles. I'm not even sure I want to know what else he did."

"No, you don't. Trust me."

Undated diary entry

Even though we have now been separated since April 12, I still have days where I am overcome by terror and anxiety when I have flashbacks about the abuse. Some days I can barely get out of bed and there were four days running where I didn't – I got up only to feed and walk the dogs and then went back to my bedroom. I was exhausted emotionally and physically and wondering if it was even worth living like this with the trauma he inflicted on me? I felt like an empty shell, stripped of everything about me and my life that had had any value to me. I had run out of energy to live.

About four weeks ago, I got an email from my neighbor Linda saying that the prince had contacted Evan, her husband, and talked about how he was coming back in August when the divorce was final. I asked Linda to please send me the email because I needed to know what he was planning. The local police told me to keep them apprised if I ever heard that he was coming back here. When she finally sent it to me there was a line in the message that said, "Thank God I have my Stradivarius for a rainy day. When I sell it I will build my house. . ." Really? He has a Stradivarius? When his daughter and I were going back and forth about a fair settlement, I cut and pasted the line about the violin into my email and asked her to please have it appraised and send me the value because it was likely that he should be paying *me* a settlement and not the other way around. She wrote back that he has no Strad but the whole point in my telling her that was to show her what a brazen liar he is. She must have said something to him because a few days later he sent an email to Evan calling him a snitch and talking about how he only said that to see what they were made of and whether they would tell me. Then he started bad mouthing them to Lou, saying they were snitches, not nice people, and were drug dealers. Linda sent me a message and said she "couldn't handle this shit anymore and didn't want to know about it or be involved." I told her they had to stop talking to him or engaging with him in any way – to block him on Facebook and email, otherwise he will not stop harassing them. Narcopaths typically go on the attack when caught in one of their lies. He didn't tell them that to see if they would "snitch" to me. He told them that because he is a liar and is always engaging in self-aggrandizing behavior. But sadly, I felt as though that was the end of my friendship with Linda. I understand her POV of not wanting to be involved in this ugly mess. Everyone else avoids me like the plague, too, because of things he's said and done. He's made me the pariah. He's been doing this sort of thing forever because it was a way to isolate me and make sure I had no support system to help me deal with the systematic abuse he had heaped on me for the last two decades. I felt as if he has ripped out my guts. I feel nothing but fear, anxiety, and terror. The more I learn about sociopaths and narcissists I realize that he targeted me and set out to systematically destroy me, my finances, along with my mental and physical health. If I had to use one word to describe him, it would be evil. Do I live in fear that he will be able to come back here? Yes, I do, which is why I had his residency revoked and his passport red-flagged at immigration. I am terrified of what he could do, or who he could hire to have something done to me. I lived in terror for most of our marriage. I pray for the day when I wake up and I am in peace and do not live in fear. I think that will only happen when I know he is dead.

September 6, 2016 – diary entry

I am flying apart, shattered into a million tiny pieces from the stress of dealing with the divorce. It wasn't enough stress that the documents took three weeks to get to Atlanta but then on Saturday I get a frantic email from his daughter, (who repeatedly says she is *not* acting as his lawyer, she is only helping him fill out paperwork correctly), telling me that there is yet *another* document to be filed and that is the Maintenance Agreement that when calculated, based on the fact I have more retirement income than he does, I would have to pay him $245 a month for ten fucking years. Thankfully, the separation agreement where he specifically waived any spousal support supersedes that, according to her. I'm back to having severe stomach problems and nightmares so horrible that I wake up in a complete panic and sweating profusely. I know over the years I blocked out much of the abuse in order to function. It was all tucked away in a dark corner of my mind, but it is there and surfaces when I am asleep. I remember having headaches so severe that I thought I was having a stroke, and I would cry and beg him to please stop what he was doing because it was literally killing me. He wouldn't acknowledge any of it, and now I know that he secretly was happy he had pushed me to that state because it meant I was too weak to fight back. I am soul weary, but I know this will pass. Someone said to me the other day that the neighborhood was finally peaceful after years of strife, tension, neighborhood feuds, gossip, and backstabbing that stemmed from him. He was always pitting one person against another, telling lies, alienating me from everyone, which of course was the goal. In the last four months since he's been gone, everything is peaceful. I have apologized to everyone I could about his behavior and explained to them that I had no clue what he was doing behind my back and that in no way did I condone such behavior and that I was sorry from the bottom of my heart that they were subjected to his malice and craziness. My heart is racing so fast that I feel as though I will have a heart attack. I have tried to shift my focus and muddle through the normal tasks of life but I feel as though I am slogging through knee deep emotional mud. Even after all the years I have researched narcissistic personality disorder I still can't wrap my head around the kind of abuse he subjected me to. There were so many signs but I didn't know what they meant, or what their intent really was. I have a vivid memory of sitting with him on the porch of the studio in Colorado, prattling on about how everything wrong in his life was someone else's fault. At that point in my career, I was simply too busy producing a record to even be able to focus on all his trivial complaints. I tried to break it off several times but he always called late at night and gave me some sob story for why he didn't show up when we had plans, or why he didn't do such and such other thing, and what a great life we could have together if only I would be not so hard on him, and it worked. He had that victim speech, hoovering, and future faking down to an art form. I always – albeit reluctantly – gave in and took him back. I was such a fool. I was completely naïve that people such as this even existed. And now I am paying the price. I pray that this torment ends with the divorce and that he doesn't do anything to fuck it up. Otherwise, I am not sure I will live through this.

September 1, 2016 – diary entry

He is now sending nasty emails to mutual friends and neighbors here in Costa Rica. This is the one he sent to Lou:

Subject: " Divorse"

"there's a name for you in italian infame translated it means a snitch. you are the most miserable human I have ever came across. You will sell the soul of god for a penny. well amigo, my answer is better too be dead than a snitch. from the bottom of my heart go fuck yourself. o I forgot, tell my ex I am free too fuck all the putta I want. this time she is not 27 but 80 no denture and she suck my dick like no one. I thank god I don't live in that snake pit. I will never ever set feet in that fuckt up country. all I can say long live trump and go fuck yourself. mangia merda e mori a as far as my ex ask her the name of all the psychiatrist she has seen . she is no angel. I don't give a shit. I am freeeeeeee and I never have to see any of you again."

He sent a similar email to my best girlfriend. It was so vile but all we could do was laugh at how pathetic he sounded bragging about how many times he was getting laid, how we were too old for sex, how he was going back to Italy to live in a civilized country. It was actually sad to see how desperate he sounded and how many lies he could tell in one email.

Other emails to friends stated that someone had given him a plot of land and he was getting ready to build a house. Another email said that he was in Italy where the government had given him not one, but *three* houses, and how he was happy to be back home. Yet another email claimed he was in Washington, D.C. There was just no end to the lies and fabrications and I have no idea how he could even keep the lies straight but I suppose that wasn't a real consideration.

Several days later, I got a phone call from a friend in Michigan who had recently spoken to another mutual friend in Denver. The friend said to him, "Say, did you hear about the string of burglaries they had in Idaho Springs? Sure sounds like the work of you-know-who!" The you-know-who was the prince.

September 8, 2016 – diary entry
His daughter sent an email saying that yes, he got the documents and was going today to the notary to have them executed. At first, I was relieved and elated that they would

be signed and I would be one step closer to being free from this hell. The sense of relief was so enormous that I started sobbing, thinking of how much I had to endure to get to this point. Once that subsided, so did the elation because until I see the actual signed settlement agreement, especially where he waives any spousal maintenance or future rights to my intellectual properties, I will be riddled with anxiety. It would be just like him to uncheck the box that waives those rights and try and go for the support he thinks he can get out of me. He has to know that I will fight that. It's enough that I have to give him a cash settlement. I am hoping that my trust in God and the universe will be in my favor and that he won't try any dirty tricks but knowing who and what he is, I have to be prepared for the worst. The anxiety is crippling. I've had to take Xanax every night for the last four nights otherwise I lie in bed and feel as though I am going to die from a heart attack. I want to scream, throw things, tear at my hair, run through the streets screaming – that's how all of this makes me feel; that I am only a hair's breadth away from going completely insane from the stress he has put me through. This afternoon I wrote him a letter that I plan to send to him as soon as I know the date on which the divorce is final. In it, I tell him that he is a con man, a demon, an evil manipulator, liar and thief, that he was nothing but a predator and a parasite, a piece of Eurotrash looking for his next victim he could screw out of money. That I wound up being nothing more to him than just another name on the long list of people he has been terrorizing, blackmailing, extorting, and intimidating for twenty plus years over money he believes he is owed. That all I was to him was a supply. I also told him that the reason I hated having sex with him is that he had reduced it to another bodily function like pissing and shitting and that I regret that I ever let him touch me. As bad as everything else is, the lies, the manipulation, the theft, the horrible things he said and did to me, letting him have sex with me is the thing I hate him most for. I have nightmares about it – and he has made it so I don't think I can ever trust anyone enough to have sex again. After all, I trusted him and look what it got me. I can't even adequately describe the feelings I have for him – loathing doesn't even come close, hatred is inadequate. Disgust and revulsion are too mild. I pray that this will go smoothly tomorrow and that when his daughter sends me a copy of the settlement agreement that it has not been altered and that we can proceed as we agreed.

STRAIGHTENING MY CROWN

November 10, 2016 – diary entry

I AM FREE!! The judge's clerk just called me to tell me that the judge signed the divorce decree and that I am now officially divorced. I was giddy with delight. I thanked her profusely for taking the time to call me with such good news. When we hung up, I walked outside onto the terrace and yelled, "YESSSSSSS! I am FREE!"

Not five minutes after I got off the phone with the court my book publisher called me to tell me that my title had been uploaded on Amazon and that it should be available for purchase later today. I felt so relieved because now if I earned one hundred dollars or one hundred thousand dollars on that book, every cent would belong to me.

Today was also my last appointment with the dentist who had done six months-worth of restoration work on my teeth and jaw. For all the years that I had lived under unbearable stress and trauma, I had nearly destroyed my teeth from clenching my jaw so tightly at night. It cost me thousands of dollars to have this work done, but now I had a beautiful smile, a new version of my book, and the beginning of a new life!

After spending an hour or two just soaking up all the good news, I was bubbling with excitement. To celebrate, I got on the internet and booked a flight to Guatemala for April. I am so blissfully happy that I can hardly contain myself. It was all behind me now.

Christmas Day 2016 – diary entry

This is the first peaceful Christmas I have had in twenty-five years. Every other holiday was fraught with stress and turmoil thanks to him pitching a fit over something two hours before dinner was to be served and putting the undue burden on me of having to pretend that all was okay when I really wanted to put a stake in his heart. It wasn't just Christmas, either. It was almost any holiday or event where I was expected to perform under the most arduous circumstances. Narcissists thrive on ruining holidays. It doesn't matter which one. They simply cannot stand seeing someone enjoy themselves, or be happy, or having a good time. Their goal is to create chaos and misery so that holidays become things to fear. I can honestly say that I am happier than I've ever been in the last two decades. I am ecstatic. I am at peace in my own house, in a place I love living, surrounded by all I really care about – my dogs, friends, nature. Nothing else really matters to me anymore.

Undated diary entry

He crosses my mind only occasionally now. No longer do I wake up in the middle of the night wondering what shit storm he has planned for me in the coming days. I sleep like a baby, no nightmares, no tossing or turning, or grinding my teeth. The only thing I am really grateful for is that I had the tenacity to continue with my plan even as he was trying to undermine me at every juncture.

I'm sure he thought if he just dug in his heels and refused to help me build this house or expedite any of the details it took to make the move to Costa Rica that I would give up in defeat. What he didn't understand is that I don't give up, and no and can't are not in my vocabulary. Now I have everything I set out to acquire thirty years ago. Maybe he was part of the grand scheme of how I was going to accomplish all these things; I can never know, but I do know that I did it in spite of him. He thought he was going to win, but he didn't understand that I never give up on my dreams.

A wave of contentment washed over me last night as I was fixing my lobster risotto for dinner. I realized that I could do whatever I wanted whenever I wanted and nobody can say a damn word about it. My life is finally my own, without any encumbrances or obligations to any other person. I am only responsible for myself at this point in my life, for however many years I have left. I plan to make the most of those years by devoting my life to writing and immersing myself in Latino culture. Already I feel incredibly distanced from the culture I was born into; and the longer I am here on the isthmus without going back to that place, the more I realize I was never meant to live there. I thank God every day that I have survived this experience. Now all I hope for is good health and happiness for my remaining days.

April 12, 2017 – diary entry
It has taken me all of this year to recover from the hell he put me through emotionally. But not only that, it has taken me this entire year to clean up this house and get rid of the crap he left he me with – every single drawer, shelf, cabinet had to be cleaned out and reorganized. There wasn't one single thing that wasn't a complete mess. I gave away every piece of furniture in his bedroom, had all new furniture custom-made, repainted the room, hung new curtains, hung

new artwork. It looks lovely – very peaceful and calm. I have finally finished the task of putting this house back together again as it was when I first moved in here by myself. I had new gates installed on the dining room door, had the yard fenced for the dogs, installed the wrought iron gate in the hallway as another security measure, and had shelving installed in the closet area which doubles as my work space. The barren patch of dirt that was the lower part of my lot was landscaped and sod was laid – nearly 2000 square feet of it. It now looks like a beautiful and serene park instead of a patch of rutted dirt. It has been a constant struggle to maintain equilibrium when my world was gyrating completely out of control. Thankfully, I was busy morning til night working on the house and editing my novel. If I had not had those things to keep me occupied, I sure would've gone insane.

ARISE FROM RUINS

April 21, 2017 - Six months and ten days after our divorce was final

It's four in the morning. Still pitch-black outside. A distant cacophony of birds heralds the coming dawn. I awake slowly and orient myself to my surroundings. There's a chill in the air and I pull the down comforter up around my ears and bury my face in the pillow. I am in the house I've come to refer to as my second home, in a city in which I do not live, in a country 800 miles away. I slept through the night without being awakened by nightmares, or gripped in fear from nowhere, or the persistent ruminating thoughts of the abusive husband from whom I am now divorced. This is the place to which I ran twice a year for the last five years in a desperate attempt to gain some normalcy in my life. It was a place free of memories, reminders, and remnants of the life I had spent with him – a life fraught with deceit, lies, dishonesty, threats, intimidation, extortion, crimes, infidelity, and probably a long list of other things about which I still have no knowledge.

For the first time in many years, I woke up and was not soaked in sweat. My face and neck did not hurt from clenching my teeth and I did not have the sense that I was falling through space with no bottom in sight. I am lying in the big brass bed waiting for the crack of dawn so I can see the top of the volcano from my bed. I relish the solitude and the quiet of the early morning with only the birds as my companions. I feel relief, peace, and calm.

Nobody spends twenty-five years with a narcissist/sociopath without being permanently damaged. Twenty years ago, I was diagnosed with post-traumatic stress disorder. The wagging finger of blame was pointed at a hundred different reasons but the truth was that I was a victim of psychological abuse and torture: withholding affection, refusal to make eye contact, verbal abuse, screaming and yelling, gaslighting, avoidance of any emotional connection, stealing my jewelry and other keepsakes, constant lies and deceit followed by profuse apologies and promises to never do it again, veiled threats of physical harm, and finally the outright extortion for half our assets. When I filed for an order of protection in May, 2016, I told the judge, "This was not a marriage. This was a hostage situation."

How did this go on for so long? Within just a few years of entering this relationship, he became so entrenched in my life that ending it was impossible without sustaining huge financial losses. In retrospect, they might have been less than what I suffered from the financial abuse he inflicted on our lives in succeeding years – bankruptcies, foreclosure, repossession of car, tax liens, bad business deals, drug deals gone bad, and writing checks that became my responsibility to cover. I believe I have finally regained a sense of self in a world I had deemed to be gyrating completely out of control. A world so permeated by anxiety and fear that I was terrified to be farther than five miles from home lest some unknown and unpredictable event happened that would endanger my safety – because feeling unsafe was the only thing I had known.

Waking up this morning, I knew I was safe. I knew nothing was going to happen to me here. Once that realization took hold, I was engulfed by a calm that I had not known in two decades. I was in control of my life and could do anything I wanted, anytime, anyplace, with anyone I chose. I did not have to live in fear of condemnation, criticism, isolation, the silent treatment, nor did I have to walk on eggshells or listen to the litany of lies I was told on a daily basis.

When the darkness receded and the first light of dawn cast its shadows across the inner courtyard, I padded to the outdoor kitchen and made a pot of coffee – dark, rich, local coffee. I stood in my bare feet on the cold tile and gazed at the horizon – a volcano to my right, and the encroaching sun directly in front of me. I was home. Not in the sense that I was in my own house, but rather the feeling that I was once again at home in my own self. The torturous last year, beginning on my birthday, which I celebrated in this exact same spot by making the decision to definitely end a relationship from which I sincerely believed only one of us as going to survive, was over. This place, to which I ran in March 2016 for safety and sanctuary, had given me the strength and perspective to plan how to end it and endure the process.

This morning was different. A sense of accomplishment washed over me like a gigantic tsunami. I stood in its curl and felt the peace and joy that was my life prior to becoming a victim of narcissistic abuse. The sun is spilling across the courtyard to warm the tiles of the old colonial house. I am sipping my coffee and feeling lighter and brighter than I ever have. It was not easy and there were days when isolating myself from the world was the only thing I could do to get through that day, but I have finally resurrected myself from the ashes of the incendiary marriage that sought to destroy me. Yes, this place is my second home because it was here that I found myself amid the literal and figurative ruins of time and nature.

June, 2017

I still have nightmares, but they are getting less and less frequent. Some nights I actually have pleasant dreams. I had to get a script of Xanax because there were some nights I was afraid to shut my eyes for fear of what my mind would conjure up that I had not yet worked through. Sure enough, a half dozen incidents bubbled to the surface and now I finally understand what they meant. They were frightening realizations. The most sobering realization that I have had to grapple with is accepting that I fell in love with an illusion – someone who never existed. Those beautiful days that we created in the beginning during the honeymoon phase were just a twisted way to control me. I devoted my heart and energy into manifesting the impossible life that he promised me. But it was his silences, verbal assaults, the cheating and the lies, the secret life he led that created the most damage. His manipulative techniques were brutal and relentless and were designed to crush my self-esteem, my mental health, and undermine the world I thought I knew. At least I will never have to endure the frigid silence or the nasty comments designed to wound me on the deepest level. The enduring pain I feel is knowing I loved a ghost, a fabrication, a lie.

Am I ashamed that I was fooled so badly? Not at all. Do I regret loving such a despicable person? No, because it was all I knew how to do. I have always tried to be an honest, kind person and a source of unconditional love. If I hadn't been that empathetic person, he would not have chosen me. I may never recover from the financial battering he inflicted but for now I am okay. I've had to sort out bigger and worse messes during my time with him. Even though I have blocked his phone numbers, blocked my email accounts, and Facebook page, and destroyed or eliminated anything that reminded me of him, I know that I will never truly be safe and will have to maintain that vigilance for the rest of my life. The damage he inflicted on my life is permanent.

December 31, 2017 – diary entry

When my Colorado Magic Jack number rang at six thirty on New Year's Eve morning, I knew it could only be him. The last time he called was late September, and the time before that was April. Both times he hung up and never left a message. A minute and half later, I heard the familiar notification sound that told me I had a voicemail message. I was enjoying the peace and serenity that had come into my life when I cut off all contact with him. In fact, when I woke up on this New Year's Eve morning, I was reveling in the idea of the wonderful paella dinner I would fix myself later in the day, a movie, and an early night to bed. I was feeling downright blissful – until I listened to his message.

It started out with "I hope you get this message. You have thirty days to stop using my family name otherwise I am going to take all your medical records from the hospital and plaster them all over your town. I had them translated by the consulate. I also want you to pay me one-half of all the royalties you received on your first book. I am no longer in the United States, and I will fight you."

That's a toned-down version of his hate-filled rant peppered with all manner of threats that went on for another minute. In 2004, he insisted I change my last name to his, and now he was acting as though it was something really precious, even though it was as common as spit in Italy. This was typical of messages he had left for other people over the years. Vague and sometimes not so vague threats to their reputation, business, character, etc. Nothing was off limits for him. Let's start with the blatant lies: The call came from his Colorado cell phone so he was not out of the US. In our divorce settlement agreement, he signed off on all of my intellectual properties in perpetuity, meaning of course, that he has no claim or right whatsoever to any book royalties I received. As for using his name, there is no law anywhere that he can invoke to make me change it and if it weren't going to be a complicated process of getting the documents certified, apostilled, and then translated (all at great expense that I have estimated to be somewhere around $800 for a sufficient number of copies to satisfy two governments and a half dozen other entities) I would change it. And even if I did change it, his reign of terror wouldn't end anyway.

I spent the rest of the day in a slump trying to figure out how to deal with this. Finally, after lunch, I hammered out a short email to his daughter and sent her the voice message and asked her to please tell him to stop calling me and just leave me alone.

After I told a friend about his message, he replied, "Oh, he's blackmailing you." I Googled blackmail and extortion and discovered that in Colorado it is a felony and has a prison sentence of two to six years and/or fines up to $500,000. The following day, I called the sheriff's department in the county where he lives. They had me fill out an online report. Then I called the District Attorney's office and told them I was being blackmailed by my ex who was calling from a Colorado number to my Colorado number, which went through the internet. They told me to file a report with the internet crimes division of the FBI, which I did.

February 2018 – diary entry

He called again but it went to voicemail. The message basically said that he had reported me to the IRS for not paying taxes, then he rattled off a mishmash of other bizarre infractions that I supposedly committed, and how he wanted me to pay him more money or else. I contacted the FBI once again and filed a report and sent them his voicemail documenting the blackmail. Then I sent his daughter an email and told her to tell him to leave me alone, that I was done being threatened, intimidated, extorted, and blackmailed. Her response was, "I wish the two of you would stop communicating with each other." What the hell? The best part is that Magic Jack finally introduced a function that allows the blocking of phone numbers, and his was the first one that I entered. Good riddance.

It's now obvious to me that he attempted to burn my house down on two different occasions. Prior to these incidents, he was always talking about the insurance money and how much I would get if the house burned. I made it perfectly clear that I would get nothing except the replacement cost to rebuild the house. I didn't realize at the time that he was fishing for information.

The first fire happened in 1998. We were headed to Denver. We got in the car and he was smoking a roach. I hated driving with him when he was stoned and I told him to please put it out. He rolled down the window and tossed the burning roach into the driveway which was lined on both sides with dried grass. It had been in the 90s during that week and everything was tinder dry. He was hostile the entire way to Denver. On edge. Driving erratically. He wanted to go to the mall to window shop. I told him that it would be better to go after my appointment when we didn't have to rush. He bitched and moaned about how it was always about *me* and *he* wanted to go to the mall. I finally relented and he drove aggressively, weaving in and out of traffic, honking the horn, tailgating, flipping off other drivers. By the time we got to Cherry Creek I was a nervous wreck.

When we got back home, I saw that the grass growing up the hill towards the house was completely charred. Within minutes of entering the house, the phone rang and it was my neighbor, telling me that there had been a fire and the only reason the house didn't burn down was that the head of the volunteer fire department lived directly in front of us and the fire station was only a few hundred yards down the road. They put out the fire that had gotten within ten feet or less of my house. It burned the hammock I had strung between two pine trees. The trees were scorched where the flames had licked the bark.

The next year, I bought a fireplace insert. It was an expensive cast iron model with a porcelain filter that heated to over 1000F to burn off any creosote before it could accumulate inside the chimney, the build-up of which could start a chimney fire. The problem was that when this catalytic converter was working, it also created a bit of smoke if you opened the insert door too quickly before it had a chance to go up the flue. His decided that this was useless. We argued, my argument being that it was a safety feature, especially since we were burning pine which is notoriously filled with resin. His argument was that it was a pain in the ass and not necessary. He took it out.

One cold winter day, he lit a fire. I was standing outside on the deck and noticed white smoke coming from the chimney followed by flames. I screamed and ran back inside and called the fire department. Then I ordered him to go outside and get the hose and get on the roof and put water down the flue. He moved in slow motion. I connected the hose for him and got the ladder. By the time he was up on the roof the fire trucks arrived and put it out. Rather than being overjoyed that we didn't burn the house down, he was pissed off. We never lit another fire again in that fireplace.

Then there were all the times he left the gas on but without a flame. I can't even remember how many times that happened, until I finally banned him from the kitchen. We used to have notes pinned to the front door that read

"CHECK STOVE – MAKE SURE GAS IS OFF" He had told me early in our relationship about how easy it was to start a fire – just leave a pot of something on the stove long enough and it would eventually burst into flames.

Right after the split, I had an email exchange with our former neighbors who had moved to Mexico. When I told her about the prince's atrocious behavior, she said, "I never wanted to tell you this, but he made a threat to me one day after we had an argument about my dog lunging at your dogs during the morning walks. He told me I should be careful, that he knew how to cut brake lines in a car."

My stomach dropped to my feet. "Why didn't you tell me?"

"What was I supposed to say, especially if you didn't believe me? There were other factors, but that was one part of why we left."

"I'm so sorry," I told her. "I understood now why you never talked to us after that incident. I, too, had been terrified of driving my car while he was still in the country especially after he made the comment that he could hire a hit man for $100."

I still have the occasional nightmare or epiphany about things he used to do that terrified me. Things that were too terrible at the time for me to process. This incident happened in 1993 or1994. We were headed home around 8 PM; it was winter, and a snow storm had just started. Suddenly, he turned on a dirt road.

"Where are you going?"

"Taking a shortcut."

"Why? It's snowing like hell and we need to get home."

"Don't worry," he assured me.

"Please don't do this. Let's go home the normal way."

We were on a desolate road and the snow was coming down heavily. Yet he persisted. The road went up a mountain and the higher we got, the heavier the snow was. It was a narrow mountain road, no guardrail, no lights, no houses, nothing. We were in the middle of nowhere. The windshield wipers could barely keep up with the snowfall which was accumulating on the sides of the windows, and the rear-end of the car was fishtailing in the deep snow. I started hyperventilating and yet he kept driving.

Finally, I yelled at him, "Stop the car. Pull over to the side of the road; I don't want to go any further. Look at this! It's dangerous and we're in the middle of nowhere." I jumped out of the car and started to throw up. I was terrified.

He screamed at me, "Get in the damn car!"

"NO! Turn this car around and then I will get in." I was sweating from fear and now I was crying, too. I can't help but wonder what his intentions really were. Was he going to leave me up there? Was he going to kill me? Was he going to push me over the side of the mountain where I wouldn't be found, if ever, until spring? I have no way of knowing now or then what he really planned to do, but I know he wasn't just taking a shortcut home.

In April 2018, it will be two years since I threw him out of my house. In those two years, I have not vomited once. The significance of this is that for the previous five or six years, I vomited all the time. I was not sick, never had symptoms, never had a queasy stomach, nothing. But at least once or twice a week, whatever I ate would not stay down. It would come on suddenly and I would run to the bathroom and puke up everything I had eaten. Then I was fine. The first couple of times I thought maybe I had eaten something that had gone bad, but that wasn't the case. After a couple of years of this, I had a dream that he was poisoning me. It seemed so far-fetched and crazy at the time that I pushed it to the back of my mind. And on top of that, I had no proof. We pretty much ate the same thing, and I did *most* of the cooking. Finally, I decided that he could not cook anything at all and I did *all* the cooking. He never threw up. Only me. Yes, there was stress, but it wasn't nearly as bad as other times and I never threw up then. I wondered if it was because he hadn't washed fruits or vegetables so I made sure that this was done ritualistically. The first year that we were separated, until the divorce was final in November 2016, I never threw up once, and the stress during that period was a hundred times worse than any previous period. In a recent dream, he was putting minute amounts of poison in my food or drinks. There were women on my narcissistic abuse survivor forum who also said their husbands had poisoned them over a long period of time, or drugged them with sedatives. It wasn't such a crazy notion after all.

Undated diary entry
Repressed memories are memories that have been unconsciously blocked due to the memory being associated with high levels of stress or trauma. Clearly, the memory that popped into my head just a few days ago falls into this category. I had not thought, even for one second, about this incident that happened in 1996, and its sudden appearance in my consciousness sent me reeling. It surfaced along with the same terror, fear, outrage, and anxiety I had when I discovered he was about to abandon me.

Over the years, the prince had received numerous job offers in far-flung places – Washington, D.C., Dubai, Malaysia, and now Florida. When he announced to me that he had to go there to meet with a friend from D.C., I said I wanted to go, too. After all, it was November in Colorado and getting out for the winter seemed like a great idea. Besides, I was not happy about him driving our only car all the way to Florida, leaving me stranded in the mountains without transportation. Many hours of discussion later, it was decided that we would simply close up the house, pack up the car, and go on a road trip. After three days of driving through treacherous weather conditions in the Midwest, we arrived in Sarasota. The only place we could find to stay because of the dog was a small motel, several notches below a Motel 6. That was fine, because it was temporary. I had already lined up small apartments for us to look at that were available right away. After several meetings with his friend, it seemed that everything was progressing and the prince was optimistic that this would be a good opportunity for him.

We ate in all the good restaurants to check the competition, went to the beach cities south of Sarasota, and explored the various keys with their quant villages and luxury homes. Sometimes the meetings took place at night, so I stayed in the motel room and watched television.

One morning, the real estate agent called and said we should meet to see the darling apartment not far from the beach. I was excited because the motel was certainly not the Four Seasons. During the walk-through of the apartment, I noticed he was scowling, didn't seem the least bit interested, and didn't have any questions or comments at all. The drive back to the center of town was tense. He said he would think about it and tell me later if that apartment would work. He dropped me off at the motel and went for another meeting, returning close to midnight with the excuse that he was observing the dinner and late-night crowd.

The next morning, I woke up early and he wasn't in the bed. I thought maybe he had gone for a walk with the dog, but the dog was still sleeping. I opened the door to the room and there he was, loading up the back of the Volvo with his belongings. The car was running and the driver's door was open.

"What's going on?" I asked, still not wide awake and unable to grasp the situation.

"I'm leaving!"

"*Leaving*? What the hell is the matter with you?"

"Nothing is the matter with me. I'm leaving," he said, getting into the driver's seat.

"No! Wait! You can't leave me here! Oh, my God, what are you doing? I haven't even gone to the bathroom yet, and I need to pack, and get dressed," I shrieked frantically.

"I'll give you two minutes."

In a total frenzy, I ran back inside, quickly used the bathroom, shoved my belongings into my bag, gathered up the dog and his things, and ran outside. I threw everything in the back and got in. I was still wearing my pajamas, and hadn't even brushed my teeth. He was seething, so I knew to not say a word, nor ask any questions, nor make any demands, nor express myself in any way. I sat there, quivering, as we headed north. His body language was so menacing that in order to avoid looking at him, I stared out the side window, sinking into the seat, quietly crying, and pretending to be invisible. Finally, after two hours or erratic driving, I had to get out of the car before I opened the car door and escaped to my death.

"I'm hungry and I need to use the bathroom," I said apologetically. He said nothing. I waited a few minutes and repeated my statement as calmly as I could.

He took the next off-ramp and found a diner. I grabbed a few things from my bag and dashed into the restaurant restroom to put on proper clothes and brush my teeth. The entire three minutes I was in the bathroom was hell. I was shaking from head to toe, feeling dizzy and nauseous, and terrified that I would walk outside to find him gone. Thankfully, when I came out, he was ordering coffee and something to eat. I also ordered a muffin and coffee to go. He walked out to the car and I scurried behind him, still afraid that he would take off and leave me there. To my utter shock, he suddenly acted as though nothing was wrong. I was still quaking with fear and anxiety. He never disclosed why he made such a hasty departure out of town, and I knew better than to bring it up. And it was never, ever mentioned after we got back to Colorado. It was as though the entire event had been erased. At the time this happened, I didn't fully process what he was doing and I shoved the entire experience as far down in my mind as it would go. Reliving this incident made me burst into tears and feel physically sick with the same terror, horror, and shock I felt then knowing that he absolutely intended to abandon me fifteen hundred miles from home.

Undated diary entry

And then the nightmares began. The same nightmares I have had for twenty years – that he kills me in any of the ways he has let me know he can. Burning down my house, blowing up my house, cutting the brake line in my car, rigging the car to explode. I woke up in the middle of the night drenched in sweat with my heart pounding out of my chest. I was terrified yet again. I finally had to resort to taking a small piece of Xanax to get back to sleep but I woke up four hours later with every part of my body shaking in fear. I know now that I will never be completely free of this monster as long as he is breathing. I know now that he will stalk me and haunt me and do whatever he can to ruin my life. But I refuse to let him. Enduring twenty-five years of emotional, financial, and mental abuse is all he gets out of me.

January 2018

The woman to whom the prince wrote that email telling her she was his soul mate and they should run off to Sardinia together was someone I knew peripherally. Over the years he had mentioned her and always referred to her as an old girlfriend. Sometimes she would even call the number in Colorado and if he wasn't there, she and I would have a long conversation about all kinds of things. She seemed like a really nice person and I certainly didn't view her as any kind of a threat. She was now married with a daughter and living in the UK. We eventually became friends on Facebook. As I struggled to piece together the events of the last twenty-five years, I decided I would contact her and ask her if she would share with me her experience with him, with the thought that it may shed some light on his behavior with me. She was reluctant at first because she didn't see how it would help me, but when I explained that so many things made no sense, and after being subjected to two decades of lies, deceit, and emotional abuse, she decided she would share her experience so that I would see that he had quite the history of deceiving women. I reminded her of the email he had sent her back in 2009, and asked her if she would be willing to tell me about their relationship – how it started, where it started, and why it ended.

"When I was 18 or 19, I went on vacation with my family to Mexico and met him on a beach. We spent about four days together and it was romantic and lovely. He was with friends who had a sailboat and one night there was a huge storm and the boat sank. I remember something like him saying the boat was a total write off and I said well they will get insurance money and he said it wasn't insured. Even though I was naive I still guessed that the boat was being used for something illegal. Anyway, after the Mexico trip every few months or once a year, I would get a postcard or phone call saying we should meet up. When I was in a relationship I would say no and when I was single, I said yes sometimes - then he would disappear. Eventually in 1983, I was traveling in Europe with my brother and sister and he and a friend of his decided to meet us in Venice and we went on to Spain for a few days. It was nice - no big deal though. After that I would still get the random messages from him so one of the times he suggested we get together he made the mistake of saying I could come and see him in Colorado. I said yes. To be honest I wanted to relive a bit of those romantic few days in Mexico and then carry on with my life. He was never someone that I wanted to have anything permanent with and I thought he felt the same. I got to Colorado and he and a friend picked me up at the airport and he did not seem at all happy to see me and it was all very uncomfortable. But that was just the beginning. We went to the house he was staying in with a couple up in the mountains. He said he had to go out for a bit and didn't come back until 5 in the morning. I was livid and thought it was rude beyond belief! Then the woman of the house told me he was married and had a daughter! I had absolutely no idea and confronted him when he got home. He said he was separated and his wife was a bitch! We then took a road trip to Santa Fe to visit friends of his. It was awful. The only good things I can say about that trip is we went to Ojo Caliente and 10,000 Waves which were two very beautiful places. Other than that, we hung out with friends of his and he ignored me. Everyone spoke in Spanish and I was completely left out and he was so rude about it all. We got back to Colorado and I happily got on my flight home. After that I would hear from him rarely. Strangely, I still had good feelings towards him but knew he was screwed up and a liar. Then when Facebook came around it seemed that he couldn't write coherently at all so I think I asked why and he told me about the accident and said that was why he couldn't write properly anymore and he seemed and sounded so strange in anything he ever wrote to me after that. I felt sorry for him. Then he would occasionally put something strange up on my Facebook wall so I figured out how to block him from doing that. They were just strange political posts - really strange. I am sure you have seen the type of thing he would do. Then he wrote the strange message about Sardinia which I hardly remembered until you talked to me about it years ago. I just felt he was demented and thought it was brain damage and wanted to be kind. If telling you this helps in any small way, I will be happy!"

second email

"I feel lucky I never saw his dangerous side. I just saw him as shady and shifty for the most part. After our time in Mexico I stopped believing much of anything he said. I know I told you about the way he was after Mexico - weird. I was so naive. I had a strange experience in a bar that I went to with him in Puerta Vallarta. I was only 18 or 19 at the time but we went out to a disco type bar and I think maybe we were dancing when I had an electrical jolt in my body and felt like I was in extreme danger. Not necessarily with him at that moment - but I just felt danger and darkness. I told him I wanted to leave. I have always remembered it because the feeling was so strong!"

When she mentioned the electrical jolt of fear, it struck such a chord with me. I told her I had that same feeling off and on for twenty-five years and the reason we had that terror was that we had, in fact, been with someone who was extremely dangerous.

THE DEPTH OF LIES

The depth of his lies and treachery started coming to light about six months after he had left for the US. The guy who put bars on the windows and gates on the front doors came to my house to give me estimates for doing similar iron work on the dining room door and the hallway leading to the bedrooms. The prince had always been buddy-buddy with him but I didn't realize that he had been feeding this guy a steady stream of lies and deceptions. Romeo was always polite and professional and didn't ask many personal questions, but as we were standing in the walled garden, he finally asked me what the hell happened? I told him that basically I had been married to a criminal – a liar and a thief, and that I had finally gotten fed up with the abuse. The look on his face was one of shock and bewilderment. I asked him what was wrong and he said, "Well, that is quite a different story from the one your husband told me." My interest was piqued and I asked him to please elaborate. Although what he was telling me was shocking, it wasn't surprising. Apparently, the prince had told him that this house belonged to him, that he had saved money for forty years to have enough to build it; that I basically had nothing, only a tiny pension, and that he received more than $3000 a month so he had to support me and pay all the bills. The walls of the garden started to move and I felt a wave of vertigo overcome me. I leaned against the wall for support and Romeo asked me if I was okay. I told him I was but that everything he had been told was a complete lie. That revelation paved the way for more disclosure and over the next couple of months, as people saw that I was getting my life back together, seemed more relaxed and happier, they started volunteering information that they deemed useful to me in trying to figure out what had happened during my twenty- year marriage. The lies were all the same – that he had been a famous chef, that this house belonged to him and he had paid for it, that the house in Colorado was also his, that I was essentially a nobody, had no assets, no career, no money, and that he was my sole support since I only received a tiny pension. It got better with each person I spoke to. The prince had borrowed money from our neighbors – $800 from one, $200 from another, $800 from a friend in Colorado. When I asked these people under what pretense did he hit them up for a loan, the response was always the same: He had told everyone that I was a tight-fisted bitch who wouldn't give him money to go to the dentist, or to do his artwork, or to pay his medical bills. They all felt sorry for him and forked over whatever he was asking for. They would never see that money again. To say I was shocked would be an understatement, but then it all started making sense -- why people looked at me askance, why when "his" friends came to the house they basically ignored me, why the mutual friends we had in Colorado came to the house to see him and basically acted as if I didn't exist. He had been feeding all of these people a steady stream of lies over the years and they had believed him. He even had the audacity to tell one mutual friend that he had rescued me from a mental hospital and if it hadn't been for him, I would still be there; that I was completely crazy, and had stolen all of his money; that I was nothing but a bitch and was impossible to live with. I started keeping track of what he said to whom and a pretty clear picture of what he had been doing for our entire relationship came to light. He had demonized me to everyone; had launched a scorched earth smear campaign about me, played the victim, and elicited sympathy from all he told this sordid tale to. It was quite the set-up that he created. But all of these people would soon find out the truth when I told them of his long history of stealing, lying, and deceiving people. In my last email to him, I mentioned some of the stories I had heard from people and his terse response was "they were all crazy and liars." At another time I might have believed him (as I had in the past) except that all the stories people were telling me were the same and none of these people had collaborated or even knew one another.

For many years that I wondered if he had been cheating on me, but he always, and repeatedly, assured me that he did not, would not, cheat on me; that he had been faithful the entire time we had been together. The cognitive dissonance that I experienced made it difficult for me to know what to believe, even though almost everything out of his mouth was a lie. There were too many unanswered questions – where did he go when he wasn't at home; where did he spend the night after he stormed out of the house; why did I always seem to have a urinary tract infection after we had sex? After he left Costa Rica, women were calling his old cell phone number. They wouldn't identify themselves and usually hung up immediately when I told them that I was the wife! All of these things niggled around in my head but I didn't have to wait too long for my questions to be answered.

Right after the Mario Batali sex scandal broke, a friend of mine posted an article on Facebook about Mario's escapades.

He and the prince were also friends on Facebook. My friend sent me the comment and asked how I could've been married to such a creature? The prince's comment was: "I got a lot of sex when I had restaurants. While my wife was working the day shift, I was out getting laid!"

Was I surprised? Not at all. It just meant that all of my suspicions were in fact true and it explains all those urinary tract infections.

He also posted many comments about me that were less than flattering, such as this one: "vecchia e disperata non sei una xxxxx (his surname) sei un cesso pubblico sposata 5 volte come una vera troia e ladra." Translated that means: Old and desperate you are not a xxxxx you are a public toilet married 5 times like a real slut and thief." Of course, I reported him to Facebook.

July 6, 2018 – diary entry

Today as I was coming home from the farmer's market, I noticed a high-end, white sedan parked at the first house on our road. A man and a woman were standing at the gate. I didn't think too much about it as I drove past on my way to my house. I parked the car and hauled the shopping bags into the house. Just then the dogs started barking wildly and rushing the little gate on the terrace. I went out to see who was there and the two people who had been at my neighbor's house were now standing in my driveway. I went out to greet them. They asked me my name and then identified themselves as the Immigration Police and inquired about the prince and his whereabouts. I chuckled and said in Spanish, "Frankly, I hope he's dead. But if he's not, he's probably in Colorado." I asked them why they were looking for him, especially since he had already been out of the country for more than two years. He opened the file and pointed to the order of protection, and asked if I still needed to have that in place? I responded that just because he wasn't in country, didn't mean I wasn't still afraid of him or what he could do. And that, yes, I still needed that restraining order attached to his passport in case he ever tried to enter the country. I asked if they knew about his criminal activities and they both nodded affirmatively and said they were well aware and that was part of the reason they wanted to question him. The entire time we were talking the woman had her hand on her hip and it was then that I noticed she had a gun. My eyes quickly flashed to the man's hip and he had one, too. I guess the surprise on my face was obvious so they went on to explain that they were police investigators and should I ever hear that my ex had entered the country they wanted to be notified immediately so they could apprehend him. I told them I didn't know whom to contact so the man wrote out a phone number on a little slip of paper and told me to call this private, secret number if I heard anything at all about him or if I felt I was in danger because of him. Well! That shook me up just a little bit. I came into the house and put the little slip of paper in a safe place where I could find it easily should I need to. Then I sat down and hastily hammered out an email to his daughter: "The immigration police are looking for your father."

October 1, 2018 – diary entry

In my dream I had started a relationship with a French man, who was very handsome and nice. When the prince found out about it, he came to me and said, "I heard you are having an affair with this guy. I just wanted to say that I have learned my lesson and I was hoping we could have another chance." I just looked at him and said nothing, trying to read his face and his body language.

Finally, I said, "How much of the money I gave you in our divorce settlement do you have left?"

He replied, "$250."

"Oh, so you want to get back with me so you can liberate me of more of my money, is that it?"

October 2 – diary entry

In my dream last night, I was swimming across the large lake to the other side where there was a cottage on the edge of the lake. Peter was there, going through some papers that belonged to his dead wife (who was killed in a car accident in 1994). I asked him what he was doing and he said he was going over the life insurance policies and that Dana had designated the prince beneficiary of a five-million-dollar life insurance policy. Peter suggest that I remarry the prince and then divorce him again and claim part of that five million. I was so upset at that prospect that I swam back across the lake to the other side and just sat there. I put on my rubber boots because that side of the lake was muddy at its edge. I didn't know what to do, so I got back in the lake and began swimming but my boots were filling with water and making it very difficult. Then I woke up.

November 2018

I was editing this manuscript and started thinking about all the people who had passed through my life during the time I was with the prince. Most of his friends had died over the years, but I made a mental note to write an email to Enzo and apologize for the harassment he was subjected to about the land in Baja while he was undergoing treatment for lymphoma. Right after I made a note to myself, I received a Facebook message from a mutual friend informing me that Enzo passed away in October. I'm sorry that I never wrote him that note.

Thinking about my cherished friendship with Teddy, I realized that I owed him a note of thanks for having been so supportive of me during a particularly stressful and traumatic period. I searched his name on Facebook and found his page, but there were no recent postings so I Googled him and discovered that he had died of a sudden heart attack in December 2017. I will always regret that I never got in touch with him after leaving the United States.

The bottom line is that my marriage was a farce, a sham, and a masquerade based on my money, social position, and empathetic nature. I was not a woman who was dependent on a husband for health, peace, joy, inspiration, guidance, love, wealth, security, happiness, or anything in the world. I had all those things. I wanted a life partner til the end. And it was for that reason that I tried for two decades to fix something that was simply not fixable. We wound up divorced because there never should have been a marriage. For twenty years, I lived a lie. The truth is that people such as the prince are monsters who try to enslave you and make you do their bidding. Appeasement never wins and in fact, it was used against me and to my peril.

One reason narcissists and sociopaths are so successful in executing their reign of terror is because healthy people can't wrap their minds around the fact that people such as this even exist.

In a relationship with a narcopath, you wind up feeling like a worn-out puppet, tethered to a person who controls you through their emotions. You have to be mindful of everything you do and say even though they have the freedom to do and say anything they want. You have to tiptoe, acquiesce, sacrifice, and always be obsequiously attentive. Your free will has been hijacked. Manipulation doesn't even begin to describe what you've experienced. All of their tactics remind me of this old fable: Once upon a time, a woman was picking up firewood. She came upon a poisonous snake frozen in the snow. She took the snake home and nursed it back to health. One day the snake bit her on the cheek. As she lay dying, she asked the snake, "Why have you done this to me?" And the snake answered, "Look, bitch, you knew I was a snake."

This is your life with a narcopath.

No good deed goes unpunished.

ACKNOWLEDGEMENTS

There are way too many people who helped me recreate the life I lived from 1990–2016 to thank individually, but if I knew you, or you knew The Prince during that period, you are probably included in this book. Most names have been changed and identities disguised, albeit loosely, to preclude retribution. I am most grateful to those who shared their past experiences with The Prince, which helped me understand and see consistent patterns of abusive behavior for decades before I came into the picture. I could not have written this book without you. I owe another debt of gratitude to other victims of narcissistic abuse who shared their stories as a way to help others understand their experience. You are a brave lot!

And finally, a special thank you to my dear pal, brilliant writer and restaurateur, Alexander Ferrar in La Antigua, Guatemala, who suggested the book title and created the cover.